I0528251

NOTES TO SADHAKAS

NOTES TO SADHAKAS
HOW DHARMA WORKS
IN EVERYDAY LIFE

Written from Cloud Mountain 2000–2001

Yogacharya David R. Hickenbottom

Editor: Ruth M. Lamb, Ph.D

The Cross and The Lotus Publishing
Camano Island, Washington, USA

Notes to Sadhakas: How Dharma Works in Everyday Life
Copyright ©2022, The Cross and The Lotus

All rights reserved. No part of this publication may, for commercial benefit, be reproduced, distributed, or transmitted in any form or by any means, including photocopying, recording, or other electronic or mechanical methods without the prior written permission of the publisher, except in the case of brief quotations embodied in critical reviews and certain other non-commercial uses permitted by copyright law.

For permission requests, contact the publisher at:
http://www.crossandlotus.com/contact.html

ISBN: 978-1-7355535-6-6 (softcover)
ISBN: 978-1-957811-14-7 (eBook)

All photos courtesy of Carla Hickenbottom Portfolio

Edited by Ruth Lamb

Book design by Jan Westendorp/Kato Design and Photo (katodesignandphoto.com)

Cover design by Rob Landers, Ruth Lamb, and Jan Westendorp

Printed and bound in the USA

Published by
The Cross and The Lotus Publishing
Camano Island, Washington, USA
Website: www.crossandlotus.com

CONTENTS

FOREWORD

The search for the sacred has been with humankind since the beginning of time as shared in the earliest transcriptions from ancient sculpture, cave art, and writing. Yogacharya David (1954–2019), a Western man born in Washington State, USA, dedicated his adult life to the search inward, constantly seeking to reawaken the highest order of sacred, spiritual-universal connection with the cosmic Divine. Here is a brief introduction to the man and the yogi, stated in his own words as much as possible.[1]

Throughout the ages, great masters have spoken of the sacred climb to access Divine-realization, to connect humanity with the highest truth of existence. Yogacharya David, even as a child, knew there was more than "surface life," or what could be experienced through the five senses. He sought answers through the church as well as through science and philosophy. Then he found a teacher who spoke a new language, one of such deep inner awareness that a whole world of freedom began unfolding.

David reflects:

> My life is a dedication to God. In fumbling steps and in the precision of movement, I steer my life toward that precious Goal. My Great Guru set the course, direction, and Goal. She beckons me still from her deeper life. God awakened me to that purpose when my own will would have taken me to self-destruction, or at best, to a mundane, senseless life. I pretend no greatness, nor even goodness, for there is none other good than my Heavenly Father. Truly, I can say wholeheartedly that it is by God and Guru's Grace that I have found my Self.

---

1   This Foreword, or a similar version, is designed to introduce the reader to David the man and David the Yogacharya and is placed in David's books in order to provide context.

I suppose it is natural to want all the world to share the sacred mystery that I feel, and it would be sheer arrogance to assume that no others do. But there is the song-bird within that bursts into Divine verse and aches to share that deepest Intimacy.

In 2007, David wrote an autobiographical sketch. He told the story of a young man in search of something of vaster meaning than he had so far discovered. Excerpts from this sketch place his writings and teachings into context as he takes us with him on his magnificent, challenging journey up the sacred mountain. The full autobiography can be found on The Cross and The Lotus website at: www.crossandlotus.com.

When David was nineteen years old, he had a tremendous experience:

I remember sitting under the stars on a warm summer night; it was around midnight. The stars were spread like a carpet of tiny lights above; my heart felt like it was physically breaking right down the middle. I felt a crushing weight pressing down on me and I was breaking under the strain. It was all too much for me and I made a spontaneous prayer in my agony, "Oh God, I don't know if you exist, but if you do, if I have never needed you before, I need you now. Help me!"

Amazingly, with that prayer came an instant relief. I felt that a thousand pounds of weight came off me in that moment. The tremendous pain in my heart was soothed. I was aware that in a split second, the agony I had been feeling was gone. Immediately after this unseen help came to my aid, my mind began to reason, "Well, since I prayed to God, my mind imagined getting some help and I felt relief as a result." It was my mind, not anything else, that helped me. No, it was more than the mind. I had connected with something wonderful and powerful and definitely beyond me.

David had other search experiences, but here we focus on his being invited to a talk by a wise "grandmother." David says:

> Well, this "grandmother" description did not appeal to me. But... eventually, I said yes. On a Wednesday evening in March 1974, we all piled into a car and drove to a nice home in North Seattle... Mother Hamilton began to speak with such spiritual power that I felt as if my long hair was being blown straight back. She spoke of God, of Self-realization, Christ-consciousness, and renunciation. Many of the concepts were foreign to me, but I recognized that this was someone who spoke with authority and wisdom. After the talk, Mother gave each of us a hug. As I stood in line waiting, getting one person closer to Mother, my heart was beating so hard I could feel it thumping in my chest. After I hugged Mother, I remember little until I found myself sitting in the back seat of the car... Each time I came to hear Mother speak, I wondered if I would feel the same power of God, and each time it proved itself true... Before meeting Mother, I would be looking for the nearest exit if someone started speaking about God, but when Mother used the word, I knew there was a new and enlarged meaning.

David speaks of initiation into Kriya Yoga that spring. He shares, "I felt I had the means for making spiritual progress, something I could take with me everywhere. How I made contact with one of the greatest masters this world has ever seen is a great mystery to me. Every day, I thank the heavens for this greatest of gifts, a sense of gratitude that does not diminish with time, but only grows sweeter."

David's Guru, the Reverend Mother Yogacharya Mildred Hamilton (1904-1991) met Paramhansa Yogananda (1893-1952), whom she affectionately called "Master," in 1925. At that time, she had been seeking deeper meaning in her life and spiritual guidance towards a truth she intuited was available but hidden from her view. Her first meeting with Master was in Seattle, Washington, USA. David said: "At that meeting when Master looked at Mother, she experienced a shock that went through her entire being."

Over time, Mother Hamilton became a Center Leader, then a Reverend, and finally, in front of thousands, Mother Hamilton received the title Yogacharya from Yogananda. She was the only woman to receive this honor, and one of only seven in total in his worldwide organization.

Yogananda followed the great Kriya lineage from India that came through Jesus, Babaji, Lahiri Mahasaya, and then Sri Yukteswar, who was Yogananda's teacher. Yogananda created a large organization in America. His aim was to "bring all into the spiritual heights he enjoyed in God." As David says: "This is the work of a spiritual master. A true Master makes you feel as if God is very close, very intimate, and very knowable."

David finds his way to this great lineage of teachers. He says:
> When I came to Mother, I was definitely a diamond in the rough. Not even a diamond, but more a lump of coal hoping one day to shine with light like a brightly-lit diamond!
> An inner pain brought me to the path, most unwillingly. And this inner pain kept me on the path when I would have gladly wandered away, back into the world.

In his autobiography, David speaks of the testing of his resolve and the testing of his commitment by Mother Hamilton. In 1982, not only did she invite David to give talks to the devotees, but she also asked him to speak of his inner experiences. He tells us: "I had never spoken to anyone about my deepest inner experiences except to Mother, and now she was asking me to say aloud in front of others my most sacred experiences. Mother had always cautioned against talking to others about spiritual experiences." David realized the reasons not to talk and now the reasons to talk. "Not easy, this," he says. The testing was for a purpose.

Two years later, Mother Hamilton ordained David as a minister. He agreed, thinking, "I can serve. I can serve Mother, serve Truth, be a servant of God, and serve the God that is within all people—that I can do! I found a way to be a minister." David's growth continued as he developed his inner agreement to find the Divine path. He speaks of a time in the fall of 1976 when he experienced a sudden rising of the Kundalini and entered what is called a "Mystical Crucifixion" state. He found himself living in two worlds: one the familiar, physical reality and the other a profound and difficult spiritual reality that had physical effects. Working between the polar opposites of physical and spiritual, a transformation gradually took place that changed his very core nature.

With his inward journey progressing, David accepted an ever-growing ministerial role while Mother Hamilton's health challenges increased as she continued in her resolve to serve God to her last breath. Supporting Mother Hamilton came at the same time as full-time school, full-time work, and full-time sadhana. Over time, David attended academic institutions; he received a Bachelor of Psychology and a master's degree in Applied Behavioral Science. Starting in 1984, he worked full-time as a counselor, and by 1985, he was volunteering as a mediator. Later, he was a founding partner of an innovative conflict resolution service.

Meanwhile, Mother, in planning for the continuation of the Guru-disciple lineage, told David that she was going to make him Yogacharya (teacher or master of yoga) and that she would be passing her spiritual mantle on to him. David shares: this gift "came as a deep Mystery, with inner potency and meaning that continues to unveil itself to me through the passing years. Far from feeling I deserved such an accolade, I felt deeply humbled and prayed that I would acquit myself to whatever capacity God would give me." David also says, "I, to the best of my ability, put my shoulder to the wheel of this Great Work begun so long ago."

On January 31, 1991, Yogacharya Mother Mildred Hamilton entered Mahasamadhi, a yogi's conscious exit from the body. David knew that Mother Hamilton was now in her light body. At this time, David says his task was "to find her in her universal Presence beyond the physical realm." That, plus other life decisions, led David to what he calls the "dark night of the soul," starting in 1992. David relates:

> At this time, I took a leave from ministerial duties as I felt I was in no condition to help others. I was entering a dark night of the soul. Mother described this dark night as a time when the aspirant has had almost continuous communion with God, then all sense of connection disappears. This was my case, and it was to last for two years. Meanwhile, I was working full-time, going to school full-time, working part-time in an internship, and experiencing a deep emptiness inside that had no solution but to go on. Never did I doubt God or the path I was on; what I keenly knew were my own errors, all the ways I lacked the spiritual qualities I knew that I should have, and most of all, how familiar God had been to me before, and now with the curtain drawn, how helpless I felt, wanting to get that inner Presence back. There was no joy for me, and I struggled to just get through the day.
>
> Time passed. One night I had a vision. I was walking along a path in the desert. This desert was so beautiful, green, and lush, with flowers like springtime. The path I walked on was spongy feeling and the air smelled delicious. I felt God. Oh, it had been so long! Like parched ground receiving fresh water, I soaked up the feeling of God. As I looked behind me, from where I had come, the land was charred black, the ground hard, cracked, and broken from earthquakes, the air black with soot; I knew the dark, ugly landscape I looked upon was a true representation of what I had been experiencing. When I saw it, I let out a cry of anguish for all that I had been holding in for so long! A prayer came: "Oh Lord of the Infinite, I have missed you so much. Please never leave me again." For the next six months, I gradually emerged from the

darkened gloom into a new Light. I had completed my master's degree and went on to a work in my chosen field, which was very satisfying.

One day, I received a call from some Kriyabans in Canada who were asking me to help clarify their Kriya practice, then an invitation to come and speak; there were many thirsty souls awaiting my visit. For so long, I had felt I was the last one to help others; now the Light came to me at the same time as the expressed need of others. God's ways are perfect and mysterious!

This was in 1995 and yes, David answered the "call" to engage in his ministry in a new way. Canadians got to hear David's Kriya teachings, as did Americans, and later, people in India.

David worked as a counselor and mediator until 1998, when, through a powerful inner direction, he left his professional career to work as a full-time minister. While not knowing what would come next, he gave up a position he loved and turned this new phase of his life over to God's design.

Just at that moment, Peter Schultz offered to build a tiny apartment for David. He now had a home. Then in 1998, Phyllis Victory, a long-time devotee of Mother Hamilton, sponsored him on a pilgrimage to India. Of course, one very important destination was Anandashram, and Swami Satchidananda, who was now the God-man guardian of Anandashram. There, David found Swamiji to be "an indispensable help in my realization."

Returning to America, David led a busy life teaching, holding retreats, and meeting with devotees in many cities in both the USA and Canada. He says:

On my return to America, I continued with a busy schedule of travel to work with various aspirants. Now, and after many years of fully scheduled days, I had time to simply go with the powerful stream up my spine into higher realms of consciousness. No longer was I daily crucified on the cross of vertically upward spiritual power meeting the horizontal daily demands of worldly activity. I was now free to sail into the mystical sea of consciousness without limit. One day, out of my mouth came the idea that I should spend a year in silence and solitude; again, it was an unsolicited idea that came unbidden from some unknown depth. Never before had I considered such an idea. I don't think I had spent even a day in silence, except when there were no others about. Hence, from September 9th, 2000, to September 9th, 2001, I was in silence and seclusion.

During this time of silence, I became established in an inner state of stillness that has never left me. And then, another life surprise: toward the end of my year of solitude, an inner direction came to me. The inner direction was for me to marry Carla, a devoted aspirant who had given sincere service for the last several years to the Work. I realized that this was an important decision, one I did not take lightly as it affected many people, even the Work itself.

In his 2000–2001 journal, David speaks of the levels of reflection and inner and outer affirmation he sought to determine whether this was indeed the right direction for his life. On December 15, 2001, Reverend Larry Koler married David and Carla in a marriage ceremony that came from Mother Hamilton and was based on a ceremony Master created.

In early 2002, David and Carla left on a pilgrimage to India. David and Carla made pilgrimages to India in 2002, 2005, 2007, and 2013. Between these pilgrimages, and ongoing into 2018, David and Carla traveled to different Centers. David says:

Through this Master lineage, He has freely given the very highest means for making the journey of realization. God and the masters have decreed this Work out of love and compassion for those who desire nothing less than the highest realization. Far too often, we are unmindful of the underlying Reality that gives real peace, joy, and wisdom for all, no matter a person's circumstance. Jesus and Babaji are the headwaters of this Work, Lahiri Mahasaya, Sri Yukteswar, Master, and Mother bless it, and it will shine in this world as long as there are sincere seekers who desire spiritual transformation.

David closes the autobiography he wrote in 2007 with the words: "This spiritual evolution is the greatest hope for a strained world that is too often filled with conflict, intolerance, and separation. Only through individuals gaining realization of their spiritual Reality will this world come to know its full glory in the Light of the Infinite Divine."

From 1998 until his Mahasamadhi in 2019, David, and after their marriage, with the assistance of Carla, led a busy life hosting services in their home or in those of other sadhakas, traveling to Centers in both the USA and Canada, as well as making several pilgrimages to India. He shared his teachings in the form of retreats, poems, prayers, reflections, and discourses. David gave over one thousand talks to devotees. David described his inner journey more intimately through his journals. He conducted services for marriages, memorials, baptisms, and house blessings. In the latter part of his life, he felt called to pilgrimage to nature's cathedrals in beautiful wilderness settings and to spend time in the desert, always seeking the great Stillness.[2]

David knew that there was more to life than narrow materialism and superficial personality satisfactions. He sought answers; he found a teacher and teachings that nurtured an evolutionary process to realization, neverendingly bringing him surprises and taking

---

2   *My Spiritual India* has David sharing his experiences during his 1998–99 pilgrimage to India and *Climbing the Sacred Mountain: Poems and Prayers of a Western Yogi,* features David's spiritual climb from 1978–2019. Silence: Entering the Cosmic Sea of Consciousness speaks not only of the wide range of multidimensional experiences David had during his year of silence, but also of the deep inner quietude that led to a lifelong unmovable sacred inner Stillness.

him to new heights. David shares, as few can, the intimate internal processes required when we break free from a bound, programmed reality and truly claim our divine nature. His teachings interweave, from start to finish, a process that spirals upward to great height and promise, then descends into the valleys to gather up the lost pieces of shame, blame, and shadow, then carries these wounds lovingly up to the transformative heights. It is the climb of a sacred mountain, and, as it is with mountains, there are steep inclines, easy paths, valleys, and rivers to ford; there is false peak after false peak until the grand summit is reached. This is the sacred mountain, unique for us all. Yogacharya David's teachings reach deep into our hearts and bring a higher dimensional perspective to each of us—a perspective that can take us into our own cosmic sea of consciousness, to our own potential for self-realization—our climb!

Yogacharya David

Editor's Note: Yogacharya David's words are important, the essence, the meaning, and the power, so I have changed very few words in his writings. Spelling is corrected and grammar has been adjusted as required. David's life's work comes in many forms, such as journals and a large number of writings in hard copy, other material from several computers, and there are tape recordings of talks that are currently being transcribed.

Notes to Sadhakas: How Dharma Works in Everyday Life is an integral part of Yogacharya David's year in silence (2000–2001). He wrote a journal, and in addition, he compiled *Notes to Sadhakas* to be included with his journal, and to be published separately.

The full journal of David's silent year and the Notes are together in the book, *Silence: Entering the Cosmic Sea of Consciousness.* This book includes all David's writings for *Notes to Sadhakas,* and as an extension, a selected number of stellar writings from the journal section.

A series of books from Yogacharya David's teachings and journals are available at www.crossandlotus.com.

It is a privilege to bring Yogacharya David's teachings forward to unify people of all faiths, people who seek a deeper relationship with the sacred, with the wisdom of our multidimensional self, and with the brilliant intelligence of Nature when She is honored as an important co-creative aspect of the Cosmic whole.

I apologize for any errors, omissions, and request Guru's and reader's forgiveness.

May we all put our shoulders to the wheel of this great Work—the upliftment and spiritual evolution of the individual soul, and of this beautifully-created world.

PART ONE

SADHAKA'S HOMECOMING

O Sadhaka,
Have you heard the inner music?
Have you seen the lightning flash?
These, O Sadhaka are leading you home.

Your home within,
Your home in eternity,
Your home, your very sweet home!
Won't you visit it, not even once?

But, be warned!
On that journey of a million and no miles
Storms will wreck you
And shaken will you be.

But, take heart!
You are not destroyed.
Sun replaces darkness,
And you know your true Self.

Ah, and that homecoming!
Stars twinkle their welcome, moon glows warmly;
And O, the sun, like a thousand suns it shines!
Yet neither burns nor scorches.

Angels sing thrills of joy!
When coming to your home of eternal bliss.
Once there—the way will seem as nothing,
All sorrows transform into haloes of peace.

O Sadhaka, let us journey home together,
For each is born and dies alone;
But here, we have the glad privilege
To walk hand in hand.

And once knowing our joy,
And finding it a boundless fount,
Drinking deep to our fill and more,
We gain even more joy when sharing it with all!

So be glad, O Sadhaka!
The journey may be long and difficult,
But you journey in the right direction!
And we will yet live to see your homecoming.

—YOGACHARYA DAVID R. HICKENBOTTOM

INTRODUCTION: LIVING A SPIRITUALLY CENTERED AND PRINCIPLED LIFE

Notes to Sadhakas is my way of sharing thoughts about leading a spiritually centered and principled life. A spiritually centered life is the substance of our interior workings—it is feeling God's Presence as the central part of our being; it guides, comforts, and protects us. Through inward stillness and deepened prayer, we grow in our ability to perceive that Presence.

A spiritually principled life is the outer structure or form of living: the principles we apply. The laws of the scriptures and the teachings of spiritual masters help elucidate how we should live— principles that inform us how to guide our life. Abiding by these principles purifies our mind and we become qualified for knowing the Presence of God.

The form and the substance must go together. With all form and no substance, our life may look outwardly perfect, but inwardly we are spiritually dead. The spiritual Presence without the corresponding outward congruency leads to the imbalance of the physical, mental, and spiritual bodies.

My intention and my prayer are that *Notes to Sadhakas* will help stimulate and deepen our spiritual life. It is true for most of us that spiritual growth occurs gradually—going to deeper and deeper levels of realization. One day, we may awaken to a much more profound awareness of Truth through a powerful inner experience. It is then that the same words we have heard, and we have even spoken ourselves, suddenly take on a new and insightful meaning. A devotee once said to me after having one such experience of the omniscience of the Infinite, "You have always said that God is everywhere, but God really is everywhere! Why didn't you tell me? Well, I know you told me, but why didn't you tell me!" With the principle of gradual awakening in mind, we may read the books and scriptures of realized masters throughout our entire life and continually get richer, more profound meanings—for growth continues even after we realize our oneness with God.

This reminds me of when I sat at the feet of my Guru. Mother Hamilton would many times repeat a story. She had a very particular way she would tell a story, using words as an exacting craftsman—carefully creating a marvelous and beautiful structure. If I ever repeated one of those stories back to her, getting the words even slightly wrong, she would instantly correct me. As I listened to her repeat something I had heard her say before, and down through the years it may have been several times, I would think to myself, "I want to be able to hear this story from the same level of consciousness that Mother is in when she is telling it." Needless to say, I never plumbed the total depths of even one of her stories.

In the spirit of true sadhakas, let us go deep, drinking from His unfathomable well of *living waters*—those *living waters* of Truth, Consciousness, and ever-new Joy. Let us thirst to drink them dry— but we will never be able to! His well, brimming with *living waters* enough to fill the thirstiest soul to overflowing, continues to flow as long as we are open for more. For it is His great joy to give of Himself to us through His never-ending reservoir. Never let any words or concepts take us from that prime simplicity of direct God-perception. Rather, let us use these sayings only as a means of expanding our ability to drink from that holy well.

A word on why I use the word "sadhaka" and other words of Sanskrit and Indian origin in these writings. The word sadhaka comes from India, where the science of realizing God has been brought to wonderful fruition. Here is the definition of sadhaka from the encyclopedia (Wikipedia):

> In Jainism, Buddhism, Hinduism, and Yoga, a *sādhaka*
> or *sādhak* (Sanskrit) is someone who follows a particu-
> lar *sādhanā*, or a way of life designed to realize the goal
> of one's ultimate ideal, whether it is merging with one's

eternal source, *brahman*, or realization of one's personal deity. The word is related to the Sanskrit *sādhu*, which is derived from the verb root *sādh-*, "to accomplish." As long as one has yet to reach the goal, they are a *sādhaka* or *sādhak*, while one who has reached the goal is called a *siddha*. In modern usage, *sadhaka* is often applied as a generic term for any religious practitioner. In medieval India, it was more narrowly used as a technical term for one who had gone through a specific initiation.

Hindu, Jain, Tantric, Yogic, and Vajrayana Buddhist traditions use the term *sadhaka* or *sādhak* for spiritual initiates and/or aspirants.

Sanskrit is the language of Eastern spiritual science, as Latin is the basis for many technical words in Western physical science. Many Sanskrit words simply do not have English equivalents. Also, there are nuances of meanings that are reflected in these words, which according to yogic science are conveyed through the vibration of the words when they are thought or pronounced. So, I have occasionally used Sanskrit words to add significance to these writings.

Sadhaka means one who is seeking God through sadhana, the practice of certain methods or disciplines; sadhana, sadhaka, and sadhu are all related to the word root sadh: *to accomplish.* Sadhana is the methodical search for God, whether through love and devotion, selfless service, wise discrimination, or meditation. To have the explicit goal of realizing God, merging and becoming one with Divine Consciousness, has found some of its greatest exponents in the scriptures, saints, and realized masters of India.

I would also like to say something here about how to read this, or any writing meant to take us deeper into our practice of sadhana. Words also have both form and substance—these writings have outward, practical principles, and they hold the power for awakening the Divine Presence—to connect us with our spiritual center. To get the fullness of both, I encourage listening on three levels.

First: listen with your mind. Use your reasoning mind to understand the concepts, and when you find they have merit, translate them into action in your everyday life. Not putting these ideas into action is to abort their very purpose. A principled life must be the first step in realizing God—practice is the core of sadhana. To confine yourself to philosophizing without changing your life is virtually useless.

Second: listen with your heart. Your heart is a place deeper and closer to who you really are—your spiritual essence. It is the *you* who is behind the outer mask of ideas and projections you wear for the world. To enter into the heart of its meaning is to find that place where it is intimate and personal to you.

And third: listen with your soul. That is the part of you that is connected with the universal intelligence of all that is—God. Through knowing that connection, your soul may take wings, not made of earthly wax but of heavenly inspiration, and soar in oneness with the omniscient Spirit of God.

As you listen in all three ways, I pray that we may take winged flight together, fulfilling the prayer of the great Master that reflects leading both a spiritually centered and a principled life: "Thy will be done on earth, as it is in heaven." (Matthew 6:10)

Dharma: How It Works in Everyday Life

The word "dharma" comes from Sanskrit, and like all words in Sanskrit, it has multiple meanings—for Sanskrit is the perfect language for subtle abstractions. Many times, dharma is translated as religion, righteousness, duty, or law. Early Buddhism gives slightly different shadings by defining it as truth, the *saving doctrine*, or *the way.* Later, Mahayana Buddhism translates it as the essential quality of any reality.

The short definition of dharma is **do the right thing:** abide by your morals and principles no matter the cost. In the movie, *A Man* *for all Seasons,* Sir Thomas More is placed in a terribly difficult situation in which his king, Henry VIII, wants More's support for the annulment of yet another marriage, and for the king, not the pope, to be the head of the church. As a result of holding to his principles, Saint Thomas loses his head! It is a story of a dharmic life.

Milarepa, the great Tibetan yogi, gives us his definition of dharma in his rebuke to a learned priest. As in the life of Jesus, the priestly class tried to entrap Milarepa due to their fear and jealousy of him, attempting to ruin his reputation. Milarepa answers the priest's sarcastic question on the *logic* (scriptural authority) for his way of life in this manner. I am paraphrasing:

> My dear scholar, you should try to rest yourself in the inborn Dharma-Essence instead of in words and talk. In daily life, you should always attempt to subdue your desires. Correct understanding and merit can only grow from within; otherwise, you will be driven into miserable realms by jealousy and the five klesas (poisonous cravings). So please do not ruin yourself! I do not understand the logic of your School. My own "logic" is that of the Guru, of the Pith Instructions (key instructions of the Guru), of diligence and perseverance, of remaining in solitude, of producing the Realizations and true understanding within, of the sincere patrons (teachers) with true faith, and being a genuine and worthwhile receiver of patronage. Being bound by the "logic" of jealousy and evil cravings, one is liable to experience the "logic" of hell and suffer the "logic" of pain; I do not know of any other "logic" than this.

Of course, the realized Master was pointing out that genuine dharma is drawn from following the teachings of one's guru; this leads a sadhaka to direct perception of the truth (Dharma-Essence). Direct perception of truth informs him or her on how to live his or her subsequent way of life. So, the realization of truth is at the very core of dharma—is both the way and the goal. True dharma may be said to have three aspects: 1) It has its origins in knowing that truth is derived through Self-realization. 2) This truth manifests as the universal principles and methods taught by a realized master. 3) In following these principles and methods, the aspirant realizes God through the dissolution of the ego-self (atman) and is raised into the consciousness of the Supreme Self (Paramatman). Having realized the Supreme Self, Dharma-Essence is realized and expresses itself in right action through a spontaneous flow from God.

Sadhaka—to act correctly in this world is to act upon the spiritual principles you have been taught and make yourself a living example of dharma. This begins with clarity: the real purpose for taking birth in a human body is to attain Divine-realization. This purpose requires that you do service in the world to resolve your karmic debt, and simultaneously, you make every effort for achieving Self-realization by diving deep in meditation. Direct perception of God transcends the law of cause and effect and leads you to live life as a spontaneous expression of your Dharma-Essence, or God's will.

By creating a positive influence in society and staying inwardly detached from the results, you free yourself from the web of karmic ties that have kept you bound. You do this by first learning to sail the skies of divine perception through deepened meditation, then loving and serving God in all that you do, and in all whom you meet. You practice discrimination to correctly guide your thoughts, words, and deeds—this is the sure path that leads you to inner glory and freedom.

In practical terms, you make the realization of God first in your life—before the demands of this world. By establishing your life on the *solid rock* of putting God first, you practice those spiritual principles and techniques that harmonize the inner and outer life with the highest truth you know.

Thus, you establish the basis for living that helps you to determine a good and positive work to do in the world. With a focus on highest truth, you will have guidelines and principles on which to establish lasting happiness in work, relationships, marriage, raising a family, and recreation. Like a hand in a glove, attunement with your inner life (Dharma-Essence) guides, inspires, and makes possible a successful outer life.

Your life is your religion, your dharma. To integrate your spiritual realization with every aspect of your life is your goal. You do not need to leave living a *normal life* in terms of work, family, and fun. Rather, Self-realization spiritualizes the entirety of your life—your mundane life, your spiritual life, and all that is! Your real purpose is to realize this great truth; that is the essence of dharma.

Implementing this plan to becoming fully realized is all-powerful, and applying it to your day-to-day life is, as they say, *where the rubber meets the road.* It is the practice of this religion—dharma—that must take possession of your soul. Practice of this sort does not simply mean reading "The Good Book" once or twice a day and saying your prayers at night. It is the employment of these highest of principles and techniques at all times and in all places. As you can imagine this is a commitment of a lifetime, and one, when it really comes down to it, few are relishing to take. But when you do, you are on the most fantastic journey of your life.

As Milarepa said, "My dear scholar, you should try to rest yourself in the inborn Dharma-Essence instead of words and talk." Do not be a scholar of the word only, rather seek out inspiration for right behavior from within, and in deepened meditation set sail for new horizons—persevere till you reach that which is beyond description. May God and the Masters' blessings be with you on the journey of fulfilling your Dharma-Essence.

Babaji On Faith

Yesterday, Chad[1] and I meditated in the future Babaji Grotto here at Cloud Mountain. While steeped in meditation, I began to petition Babaji with a prayerful mantra, "Om Babaji." This phrase came again and again. A desire rose up in me to see Babaji face to face—and for Chad to see the same. Babaji appeared before my inner eye. "Babaji, please come," I requested inwardly. "No, I shall not!" came the terse reply. The inner voice quoted the *Autobiography of a Yogi*, "It is easy to believe when one sees, there is nothing then to deny." He continued with a Biblical quote, "Now faith is the substance of things hoped for, the evidence of things not seen." (Hebrews 11:1)

This quote from Paul rang in my consciousness. My searching mind opened itself to know its meaning.

David: "Is there something special to be gained by going in faith?"

Babaji: "Yes."

David: "Does faith open doors of receptivity?"

Babaji: "Yes."

David: "If you came in physical form, would it add nothing to the development of needed faith?"

Babaji: "Yes."

David: "And with this perfected faith, you, or anything else, would be manifested naturally?"

Babaji: "Yes!" came the answer.

Inner consciousness has long been working on deepening my under-standing of faith. Jesus emphasized it as a central theme of his ministry. I have often wondered over this fact and the doors of understanding have slowly opened through the years. The essential problem to the igno-rant mind is that a veil of separation, obscuring the Light of Spiritual Consciousness, covers it as a shroud. The solution to this dilemma is the most pressing matter for the spiritual aspirant.

---

1   Chad stayed at Cloud Mountain for part of the year I stayed in residence.

All great religions and enduring mythologies speak to this separation of the soul from its Divine Source. The ultimate resolution of this knotted point is to pierce the veil of separation in order to directly perceive the Divine. It is observed that for the accomplishment of any great goal, faith is required. It may be the faith of self-confidence, faith in a great principle, or in a higher ideal, such as liberty, justice, or faith in the supreme governing Intelligence of God.

Faith in one's self is good, faith in a higher ideal is better, but faith in God creates a link between our self and the omniscient and omnipotent Consciousness that is the *All and All in All*. This link to God is the greatest accomplishment of faith. Faith literally multiplies one's inner and outer resources by many, many times. In fact, corresponding to the degree of faith, the individual may be a clear and open instrument for the Almighty to operate in any way the Divine wills—with unlimited potential.

Like a laser, deep faith makes the mind singular and rends the curtain of separation that directly connects the soul to the infinite Source of Being. But the mind is stubborn in its adherence to the world of matter. Deep subconscious associations to the limits of the world work against knowing Spirit. The shortcut of using faith in God to surmount attachment to matter is of great import to the sadhaka on the spiritual battleground.

Some materialists say, "If I only saw a miracle, then I would believe." But is it so? Let that one be witness to a so-called miracle and the mind would weigh, measure, and dispense with that miracle in a hurry. "It's a hoax," declare some. "It's an anomaly," say others. "It can be true for them, but not for me." Or: "They have a special gift, a power, unexplained by science, but it does not prove anything beyond a simple new discovery!" Thus, the skeptic wipes his or her hands clean of the miracle, puts it into a comfortable box, and continues on the materialistic way.

When the inner calling draws us deeper into Spiritual Consciousness, oftentimes in spite of the mind, not because of it, we come to a belief in something deeper than the ego-self and physical nature. Through our deepened communion with Spirit, the negative influence of a matter-drenched mind is gradually dissolved.

Communion with Spirit takes us beyond the human mind alone. Belief, a thought of the mind alone, is the weaker cousin of faith. **But faith is an inner knowing that transcends a belief. Faith directly connects us with a deeper reality and brings spiritual power and understanding to the fore.** The tiny firefly of human belief is easily eclipsed by the stupendous solar power of faith. Babaji, Jesus, and all the great spiritual Masters are constantly drawing our attention to the superior power of faith.

Through faith, awareness of Spiritual Consciousness deepens. We perceive a world of potential opening up. This world of infinite potential is all about us, but unseen by many. With this opening, spiritual power vibrates with new possibilities made possible by faith—bearing fruit in a changed consciousness. We realize this world is brimming with spiritual Power and Intelligence. We see clearly the Light of our own Being is connected to the very same cosmic Light that is God and which illumines all creation.

In this illumined state, we have perfect faith that this unlimited spiritual Power is working on our behalf. With deep faith and inner surrender, the supreme Power and Intelligence guides, protects, and reveals our ultimate destiny. Faith, then, becomes a transfiguring lens that sharpens the mind to be a fit instrument of Supreme Consciousness. Faith takes us to the threshold of realized knowledge through direct experience. All this, faith does when we open ourselves to its unlimited potential.

"If you have faith as a grain of mustard seed, ye shall say unto this mountain, remove hence to yonder place; and it shall remove; and nothing shall be impossible unto you." (Matthew 20:17) This is no idle promise. The fact that the demonstration of that promise is only too rare in this world does not mean it is not true. It only means that, as aspirants, we have work to do. Through prayer and deepening communion with God, we grow in our understanding and experience of faith. The disciple Peter represents the personification of an intuitive perception of truth. But even he fell short of perfect faith when he denied the Christ. Yet, he never gave up, and eventually came to have that perfect faith. Through the same kind of tenacity, we perfect our faith that leads us to be consciously one with our greater Reality, God.

My friends, receive the blessings of Babaji. Through oneness of Spirit may our faith be perfected into complete Self-realization. May that perfected faith result in manifesting the purity of Light in all we do and in every part of our life.

Om, Peace, Bliss, Amen.

Tithing[2]

Tithing dates as far back as there has been a recognition that man is subordinate to something greater than himself—God by whatever name. The tradition is to give the first fruits to God. This presentation of a gift is made to a place of worship, a deity, or a teacher. When you enact the giving of *the first fruits* to God, then you set into motion several blessings.

First: Giving the first fruits to God creates the right attitude for you in life. Through your offering, you humbly acknowledge that God is responsible for your prosperity and your ability to succeed— that He is the source of all *good fruits* that come to you.

Second: You support that which brings Light into your life through those offerings. If you receive value from a teaching or place of worship, it is incumbent upon you to support it.

---

2   The word "tithing" comes from the old English *teogotha,* meaning "tenth." To tithe means to give one-tenth of your agriculture or income towards the support of the church and clergy. Although the word tithing only goes back to Middle-Age Europe, the giving of support to a church, deity, or teacher has dated back to the earliest recorded history.

Third: You bring direct blessings to yourself. The spiritual principle says, "As you give, so shall you receive." When you give of your time, your abundance, your love, and service, then you receive accordingly in return. Life becomes dry and constricting if it is all about me, mine, and more. You open a circuit when you give in mindfulness to God; this mindfulness opens channels of connection with the Source of all that is. "Give, and it will be given to you: good measure, pressed down, shaken together, and running over will be put into your bosom. For with the same measure that you use, it will be measured back to you." (Luke 6:8) When you see someone in need, when you give to them as you would give to God, then it is very pleasing to God and His saints. Let all such giving come freely from your heart, and your heart will know the blessings of both giving and receiving.

Fourth: Has to do with putting your attention on God. Give God the "first fruits" of your thought. Chant His holy name, breathe Hong Sau, keep your morning and evening Kriya appointments, think of Him as you serve Him in others, give Him at least ten percent of your attention—the first fruits of thought going to Him all through the day. In truth, there are very few tasks that require your full attention, and even then, you can precede the action by invoking God to be your strength and to direct your efforts. With the first ten percent of your attention always on God, you can never forget Him, and by the virtue that it is your first ten percent, you will always choose to go *with* Him, never against Him.

Four Lions and The Diamond Light

(A ~~TAIL~~ TALE THAT ENDS WELL)

Going to the inward Mind
Four lions lie in wait:
Fear, lust, greed, and wrath.
Waiting, waiting, waiting, they wait!

For a moment, a weakness is perceived...
Then upon their hapless victim
They pounce to devour his very life!
The life that will make the lions to live again.

Four lions lie in wait,
Looking for a moment in time
When they catch a look, a glimmer,
Of lack of resolve gleaming in the eye!

Or doubt, it is, that creates a chance;
Perhaps loneliness, it makes them lick their chops!
They lie in wait in darkened dale
Where self-pity makes its prisoner an easy prey

But wait! The lions scurry for cover
When like-minded aspirants join in on the stroll.
And oh, how those lions detest and are sickened to death
When melodious words are sung to the Most High.

Ah! Here comes a chance, a lovely trap
When ego of pride makes stilts for legs.
Yes, pride places the head high on wobbly peds
"We will not attack 'til the moment is right,"
say those wily lions in wait!

Oh, here he comes, that aspirant riding high
Round corner too fast, head and chin tilted to the sky.
Lions on the wait on either side
For unwieldy stride to bring that one down with a crash!

And when the crash comes, as it certainly must come,
The trap of shame is sprung.
The game is theirs, the lions have won!
They suck life's blood down to its very marrow.

And when the gorging is done, (but it is never truly done),
They seek to devour corpse and all!
But deep down inside, close to the heart,
Resides a spark they can never touch.

It is a spark, a glowing Light
That is oft' clouded by gray and dark.
Is hidden, really, never dimmed;
For once uncovered, it shines brilliantly as ever again!

The lions, if they could (and they would if they could),
Take away that little diamond of Light
And devour whole: life, ego, and corpse.
But they can't, they can't! As much as they would like.

For that Light, that brilliant shining Light,
Cannot be bartered, sold, nor stolen away.
No, not even tarnished, corrupted, or even a dent will it know!
For it is forever, and that cannot be changed.

That is your treasure O aspirant!
Gems of realization and spiritual Light of gold
It is your inheritance that, no, not even you can give away.
It is a gift, and it pleases It greatly to give Its Self to you.

So those lions may be there, they can lie in wait,
But you've a secret weapon they cannot devour;
no, not even in their dreams.
You've defeated those rascal lions, you've beat them square,
You need only claim... (shall I say it) your lion's share!

Blessings from the Guru

Through the all-pervasive, all-knowing consciousness of God, time and space become principles without absolutes. Therefore, sadhakas who call on their guru in full faith, wherever that guru may be, will receive help both visible and invisible through the God-tuned Guru.

Just a small incident with my own Guru has stayed in my mind for over twenty-five years. I was traveling in the Sahara Desert, riding through a military zone on an army truck. Nothing but sand dunes for as far as the eye could see in any direction. Suddenly, there was the fragrance of my Guru's perfume she wore at that time. It came without any particular thought of her—out of the blue, you might say, and it stayed with me for many minutes. It made me know that although I was halfway around the world in a war zone, she was ever with me.

It is God Himself who has set up residence in the guru-teacher. That is, through the spiritual perfection of a devotee, God is able to use that one as an instrument of His will as the guru. Because spiritual aspirants, ignorant of their oneness of the all-beneficent Presence of God, are in need of a human example of that Oneness and these teachings, God commissions that one to serve as the guru to all whom God brings to him or her.

The faith of a devotee may be awakened through the guru, and love and devotion may be channeled to God, in part, through the teacher. The guru, being absent of ego, acts as a conduit to awaken the Living God within the devotee—therefore fulfilling a pattern set down through history. Even Jesus, coming as an Avatar, required baptism by John the Baptist, his Guru from a former lifetime.[3]

When the devotee of God calls upon the guru with awakened faith, then virtue, the healing power of God, goes out from that one. Sometimes the guru is fully conscious of this fact, sometimes partially conscious, and sometimes not at all conscious. It makes no difference, for it is the Superconscious action of God that performs what is necessary. When Jesus walked through the crowd and many were touching him for his blessing, he stopped and asked, "Who touched me?" The disciples were confused by their Master's question because so many had been touching him. He said, "I perceive that virtue has gone out of me." (Luke 8:45–46) This is a case of Jesus being partially conscious of being used as a medium of God. Isn't that marvelous! He felt virtue go out. And indeed, out of all who were reaching out to him, one had full faith and was healed.

Lahiri Mahasaya said, "If you deem it (my picture) a protection, then it is so; otherwise, it is only a picture."[4] The faith of the devotee makes it so. And, it is in combination with the God-tuned nature of the Master that it becomes a very powerful connection to Divinity indeed! The protections I have received from my own Guru are too many to count.

One time comes to mind when I was protected on the spiritual level. A popular "Guru" from India came to town sometime after I had met Mother and taken her initiation. I had gone to see him speak before I met Mother and felt nonplussed by him. It came to mind that it would be interesting to meet him now, after having met my Guru, to see how he would seem to me now. After his talk, which did not impress me any more the second time than the first time, he was leaving the place. All the devotees stood as he left. As he walked out, he stopped and looked in my direction. He was about twelve feet away. There was a parting of all the devotees and

---

3   *Autobiography of a Yogi* (p. 35).

4   *Autobiography of a Yogi* (p. 31).

there was a straight line of sight between us. I could clearly sense him psychically rummaging around in my psyche, feeling a definite invasion. The thought of Mother came to me and immediately I felt surrounded by a wonderful aura of Light. The Guru's head snapped back and he proceeded out of the hall. Sometime later, I heard that he practiced many occult powers. I gave a prayer of thanks to my Omniscient Guru for her protection. It also made me aware that although Mother had access to the most intimate parts of my psyche, I never felt invaded by her, and this gave me a newfound appreciation for the purity of her Light.

Through his or her own realization, the guru has dissolved his or her ego of separation from God and has realized Oneness with the all-pervasive Spirit of Consciousness. Then God may commission that one to play the role of the guru. That is, the guru will teach the methods for devotees to practice in order to realize their greater reality; the guru will stand as the devotees' protector on the spiritual plane; the guru will be the example of a realized person; the guru will impart the essential spark of Divinity required for devotees to become fully realized.

Even after I had several Kriya Initiations with Mother, each one had special significance, as in my enlarging consciousness I could absorb more of what she had to give. Mother had been quite ill at the time I received my last initiation. Kneeling in pronam before her, she touched me on the ajna in blessing, and the power that radiated from that touch I can still feel when I think back on that time. Such are the blessings God gives through the guru.

Because the living Presence is consciously moving through the guru and the sense of ego has dissolved, if that one is who he or she should be, then God may fully express Himself through that personality pattern. It is often the case that God uses a spiritually evolved human instrument in which the human ego is not fully dissolved, Lahiri Mahasaya, Yoganandaji, and Mother being prime examples of this in their earlier years of teaching. Highly developed in their realization, but not yet perfected in consciousness, they assumed the role of Guru by God and their own Guru's commission. In fact, by assuming such a role, it helped that one to dissolve his or her own ego by fulfilling these karmic ties. They did not assume the roles out of ego, but by inner direction and the request of their own Guru. Mother told me at the time of making me a minister that Master making her a minister and giving her permission to initiate others had helped her attain her own God-realization.

As long as the guru is not yet perfected, but making progress toward the goal, God may use that one to full effect.[5] In fact, it can be encouraging to devotees to find common ground with a highly realized guru treading the path ahead of them. The devotee will think, "I can do this also; it is not only for perfected Beings to achieve this goal!" One advantage of the guru-disciple relationship is that it keeps the devotee's attitude humble before God. Always feeling the desire to please the guru, always knowing the guru went to his or her own realization before the disciple, the aspirant keeps a humble attitude before God and Guru. This helps to prevent egotism from taking a foothold, even in the higher realms of consciousness.

Following a path or a spiritual master should not lead to narrow sectarianism, nor should it be treated as a business enterprise. As Mother used to say, "God can neither be bought nor sold." In the same way, those who teach and promote themselves as an exclusive way to realization fall short of the full truth. And there are those who follow a true Guru, and then, after the Guru's passing, treat the Guru as a product that only they are entitled to copyright and have the exclusive right to sell! True devotees are attracted to the honey of realization. They will pass the glittery show of the spiritual marketplace and be drawn to the Truth of a realized master. In this way, they will find fulfillment of their one true desire.

---

5   Meher Baba wrote that one fully established in the fifth chakra may be commissioned to be a Guru.

The guru-disciple relationship is personal. I always had a twin sense of wonder around my Guru. On the one hand, I was so amazed that there were others who were as interested in Mother as their Guru as I was, and on the other hand, was amazed that the whole world was not at her feet, so great was she in God. But whether a guru has one or two devotees they take to God, or thousands or more, the Light is just the same in each true Guru. They come as a blessing to all, even those who are not conscious of it. The guru then is a source of blessings to all whom God puts into their hearts to make it so. As a teacher, role model, and source of invisible virtue, the guru becomes a blessing in our lives that is without comparison. Realization of God being the sole aim of the Guru for the devotee, they yearn for real devotees on whom to shed the Grace and blessings of God.

Of Will and Surrender

Will

Will, or volition, is the basis for all creation. God the Father resides in His Self as formless Spirit. This Pure Spirit, transcendent to all creation, is called the nirguna aspect of God. In this aspect of God, will is at rest. When pure Spirit takes form as creation, It is called Prakriti, Mother Nature. The Shakti power of God expresses its will through the laws that govern spiritual and material creation. This created form of God and its laws is called the saguna aspect of God. Sown in every particle of creation is the perfect Light of Spirit known as the Savior or the Son of God. The will of the Savior is the preservation of Light and Its attributes in nature's creation. This makes up the trinity of the One God. For God is both manifest and unmanifest, with form and formless.

We, as human beings, are said to be made in the image and likeness of God. (Genesis 1:26) The image of God is God with form, saguna, and the likeness of God is Spirit without form, nirguna. The Supreme Being of God is the All in All. The first of these Alls is God as Spirit, nirguna, and resides as a hand in a glove in the second All, God with form, saguna. Thus, as in the inner, so the outer. As God expresses Himself in a vast cosmological sense, so does God reflect that same pattern in humanity. Since humans have the same pattern as God, they are endowed with free, creative will.

From our first movement and cry as a baby we manifest will. The cry of the newborn is *automatic physiological will.* From the beginning of this birth, children have their own distinctive personalities. This is due to vasanas, subconscious patterns from previous lives. These vasanas, combined with new patterns developed in this lifetime, create our *unconscious will;* that is, will that comes spontaneously from the unconscious mind.

As we become more conscious of the world, we learn to copy and obey those around us. This develops *unthinking will* because it is responsive only to the environment around us. The next stage can be characterized by the "terrible twos," when we learn to say "No!" We exercise *blind will* against authority, as this will is reactive only.

As development continues, and our ability to reason progresses, we manifest *thinking* or *Reasoned will.* We can observe this Reasoned will in even young children who start a creative project and reason their way through to completion. Each developmental stage adds another ability to the whole but does not usually completely replace the developmental stages of will that came before. For example, a carpenter is using *Reasoned will* to build something but misfires his hammer, nailing his thumb by accident! He reacts with automatic *physiological will* and draws his hand back with a yelp.

We can analyze our own behavior to help determine for ourselves if we have successfully developed all these stages. Many people are not fully developed in their *reasoning will* and are dominated by a lower developmental will. For instance, one may be an adult and still be ruled by *blind will* and remain eternally rebellious, automatically reactive to any authority figure. When confronted with someone who has authority over him or her, this individual will all too often quit his or her job or try to get revenge, acting out of *blind will*. Persons dominated by *unthinking will* may specialize in conforming to what is expected by others without even knowing what they themselves want and never dream of going against an authority figure.

Also, a later stage of developmental will can dominate over an earlier stage. For instance, a *blind will* may not show any *automatic physiological* response to an authority figure: i.e., a defiant child will not cry when spanked. Or a well-developed *Reasoned will* may overcome a *blind* reactive will by learning to *think* before acting instead of just acting.

Will has come under criticism due to a perception that it is used to suppress feelings. Will, in this scenario, is seen as a ruthless dictator and it is deemed necessary that it be dethroned. True, an unbalanced will can try to rule as a dictator. Of course, there are rebellions by disgruntled "subjects." These battlegrounds of the psyche often manifest in the offices of doctors and psychologists. Reason should be a wise king who listens to all subjects and then does what is best for the higher good. The rule by feeling nature or less developed wills makes for poor decisions and sometimes disastrous consequences.

When one is drawn to the spiritual path, these various types of will are usually in diverse states of development. Under different environments, each may predominate in its influence. For instance, given a predictable set of circumstances, a *Reasoned will* may be that benignly just ruler. Suddenly a threatening circumstance, real or perceived, and it triggers a *blind will* reaction that becomes rebellious and angry in a tense situation. Most aspirants on the path come with wills that are in a flux with various states of development.

Due to the fact that spiritual development represents the most powerful dynamic in human development, it is no small wonder that it represents not only the greatest hope for the individual but the greatest threat as well. The proper development of will becomes integral to the spiritual development of the aspirant. The human ego's highest form of development comes as a strong, balanced *Reasoned will*. It may have been honed in earlier development through sports, business, and artistic or intellectual pursuits. There are a number of areas in which this balance can be partly or wholly achieved.

As balanced *Reasoned will* strengthens, it brings its subjects *automatic physiological will, unthinking will, blind will*, and *unconscious will* into a happy balance. This state of affairs is rarer today than common, so a large part of sadhana, spiritual discipline, is bringing this inner kingdom of wills into balance. Any personality ruled by lower wills cannot maintain a steady state of mind required for higher spiritual advancement. Fortunately for those of us entering the path, there is also help in developing this balance by following the light in deepened prayer and meditation. Our willingness to work on *Balanced Will* is greatly enhanced by the strength gained through repeated contact with the Light within.

The next stage in the development of will comes as a transpersonal or spiritual development. Paramhansa Yogananda prayed this way:

> O Father, Mother, Friend,
> Beloved God, I will reason,
> I will, I will act:
> but guide Thou my reason,
> will and activity to the
> right thing that I should do.[6]

Buddhi, or higher reasoning of intellect, may be turned downwards to things of the world, or focused upward on things spiritual. When spiritualized, it becomes illuminated by the Purusha or the Son of God. This spiritually charged will may be termed, *Dynamic Will*. In the beginning, leading a spiritual life means learning and obeying the laws of

---

6   Paramhansa Yogananda. *Whispers from Eternity* (p. 93).

God handed down by prophets, spiritual masters, and the scriptures of religion. Using human reason, the seeker brings his or her life into harmony with a set of dos and don'ts designed to purify the consciousness from material desires and bring it to Spiritual Consciousness. The use of reason to bring one's life into alignment with true spiritual principles plays a real and valuable service for soul development. This alignment of spiritual principle and outward action is like creating the solid foundation for a skyscraper building. It prepares body, mind, and soul for deeper God-communion. If these essential principles are not exemplified by sadhakas, their attention will always be drawn back to the missing step, often with difficult consequences.

With this proper preparation, individuals are readied for deeper association with the Divine. With the indrawn attention of the intellect, Buddhi, the rays of the Light of God enlighten the consciousness. Through deepened prayer and meditation, this enlightenment may come in the form of a realization through feeling/intuition, an inner vision, a strong insertion of an idea, a voice, or a dream of the superconscious dimension. It may also come as recognition of receiving the truth from an outside source: i.e., from another person speaking, reading a book, or by observing nature. The enlightenment clearly comes from a source beyond the normal conscious workings of the mind. The entire Being of individuals can be uplifted, bringing them into contact with a sense of purity, clarity, and truth. At these times, the will is charged by *Spiritual Dynamism* and a feeling of power that transcends any of the lower wills, making one feel in touch with a vast storehouse of will and potency.

At this stage, the upliftment comes and goes. When the Light of upliftment recedes from the intellect, individuals notice a definite difference between normal thought processes and the illumination that has just occurred. An afterglow of the clarity, purity, and truth may still be hovering in their consciousness, but it cannot be fully maintained. The unillumined rational mind must then use *Reasoned will* to approximate harmony with the revelation. This is contrasted with *Dynamically Charged Will* experienced in the uplifted state or when surcharged through prayer.

When in the uplifted state, individuals feel so natural and free that it cannot be imagined to be any other way. But, because the mind has yet to be fully purified, past patterns act like gravity to pull them down, back to earthly consciousness. Returning to human consciousness from that heightened state of consciousness creates a battle between harmonizing old habit patterns of the mind with the new state of Being experienced while uplifted. A battle often ensues between lower natures of will and the enlightened *Reasoned will* in this aftermath. Maintaining a true parity will not be possible between the *Reasoned will* and the purity of revelation, since *Reasoned will* is inferior to Superconscious Realization. In the beginning of sadhana, these experiences of upliftment will seem all too rare for sincere seekers and *Reasoned will* must do its best to live according to its own highest Light of Truth. Sadhakas are tested again and again, striving to attain the higher consciousness, and experiencing the pulls of vasanas, past habit patterns. Through prayer and meditation, they are able to access the *Dynamic Will* of Spirit to overcome all limitations of the past. Sadhakas combine what they have learned of spiritual principles with inner revelation to guide their actions for further purifying of the mind. Gradually, the mind and will become more purified of lower tendencies and can grow into the greater life of *Dynamic Spiritual Will* and beyond.

Rising to the next step of will in this long journey of the soul, individuals are initiated into the mystery of the Presence of God. A spiritual master may awaken this Presence in sadhakas when they are taught the methods of deeper spiritual communion, such as Kriya Yoga, chanting the name of God, dedicating actions in selfless service, and divinely loving God. This Presence takes an active role in guiding the life of the sadhaka through *Intuitive Spiritual Will*. This will guides aspirants even in minute matters, resulting in the acceleration of mind purification, which is necessary for higher attainment. It is superior to *Dynamic Will* in that sadhakas feel as if they are but a witness to the workings of *Intuitive Spiritual Will* versus the feeling of a powerful *Dynamic Will* being operated by the individual. It is at this stage that surrender takes on an even deeper meaning.

Surrender

From the beginning of our spiritual journey, surrender plays a role. At first, surrender means subjugating the whims and desires of the ego to the Ten Commandments or the Yamas and Niyamas, those dos and don'ts of spiritually principled living. We gradually increase *Reasoned will* to bring the lesser developmental wills into conformity with these principles. This surrender of the ego through *Reasoned will* to higher virtues teaches the intellect the practical value of surrendering to a higher order than to desire nature of the ego. It also strengthens the focus of our spiritual purpose in life.

Going beyond learning and obeying a principled life, individuals open themselves to a greater interior life. This means surrendering their exclusive focus on things material to the intense desire for Spiritual Awakening. This is more demanding and exacting of them, mentally and emotionally, than following the commandments of principled living. They are indeed of greater faith now moving from the relatively safe confines of leading "a good life" to the bewildering jungles of inner enfoldment. Deeper lessons of attunement to an inner knowing become, moment to moment, vitally important to their spiritual survival. Prayer and meditation must be the precursors to this enfoldment for it to go normally. The inner laws of attunement are even stricter in the governance of behavior, and paradoxically, sadhakas feel greater freedom through surrendered servitude to the Infinite One.

Through intense sadhana, the mind and its various levels of will are brought into line with the *Intuitive Spiritual Will*. The *Reasoned will* surrenders itself completely to the higher order of *Spiritual Will*. The training previously gone through in obeying spiritually principled living is a necessary preparatory period for this greater demand of the Spirit. The soul at last has come face to face with its evolutionary destiny. Total submission of the egoistic human will to *Intuitive Spiritual Will* allows for the total transformation from the son of Man consciousness (the ego consciousness) to the Son of God Consciousness (the Spiritual Illumined Self). During the sadhaka's life, they will experience three stages of surrendered will. The first is to know and obey spiritual principles such as the Ten Commandments or the Golden Rule by *Reasoned will*. The second, through deepened prayer, gaining access to *Dynamic Will* surcharged by spiritual power. The third is the total sublimation of individual *Reasoned will* to *Intuitive Spiritual Will*, resulting in the elimination of human will as it was previously known. At this final stage, the volition of sadhakas comes spontaneously from the Divinity through *Intuitive Spiritual Will*.

These three stages of spiritual development can be likened to three ways of knowing the sun. Following spiritually principled living by studying the scriptures, reading the lives of saints, and praying to a distant God is like standing on the earth looking at the rays of reflected sunlight in the full moon. When revelation comes directly to the mind and individuals feel more and more guided by an inner light, it is like standing on the moon, looking directly at the sun. When total transformation comes into the Being of the Soul and *Divine Will* flows spontaneously through every thought and word and deed, then it is as if that Soul becomes the burning orb of the sun itself. No longer is that one looking for the Light, or being led by that Light, but that one **becomes that Light Itself**. This is the whole meaning of Jesus' life in giving up the ghost, the human individual self, and resurrecting in the Holy Ghost, the illumined one!

Individual will disappears and one becomes a witness to the *Divine Will*. The seesaw battle between the lower developmental wills and Divine Will is over. The lion and sheep lie together in peace in this united kingdom. Individuality sees itself as but a witness to *Divine Will's* play, both within and without. Free of internal struggles, the soul is a fit instrument to carry out the Divine Father's Will.

Then, with Jesus, that one may say in full awareness, "Of myself I am nothing, It is my Father who doeth the works." (John 14:10)

And what works are these? Everything! Every thought, word, and deed, comes from a singular Divine Source. This same state of consciousness may say, "I make no judgment, but if I judge it is true." (John 5:30 adapted) Does this statement contradict itself? No, not when seen in the light that the "I" is the witness, who has no judgment, but observes the flow of universal Christ Consciousness that discerns very clearly Light from dark.

The drama of Jesus' life depicts going the final mile to that total surrender. The son of Man represents the ego. The Son of God represents God Consciousness. Jesus had temptations along the way, such as in the desert after his illuminating experience with John the Baptist and his forty-day fast; the pleading temptation by Peter for Jesus not to go to Jerusalem and be crucified; and, the greatest temptation was in the garden of Gethsemane depicting Jesus' absolute submission, even unto death, unto *Divine Will.* Even while carrying the cross, Jesus fell three times, indicating the tremendous load he carried, buckling under its weight in carrying out his mission.

These are all indications of what the sons of Man can expect on their way to transformation. With unswerving passion, individuals must rise through these opposing forces. In times of temptation, they must use strong *Reasoned will* and *Dynamic Will* anchored in prayer and meditation to guide their way. It is in these very times, caught in the clutches of the opposing force, that they are least likely to feel the inner guidance. But through pure faith, they assert *Reasoned* and *Dynamic Will.* At other times, they feel the Divine Presence, a flow of Divine Guidance, and surrender to that movement. In the upward ascent, sadhakas will have occasion for the right use of *Reasoned will,* surcharged *Dynamic Will,* and full surrender to *Divine Will,* depending on the inner fluctuating states of consciousness at the time—like a dance responding to the partners they find themselves with at any one time. This dance goes on and on in sadhana until at last the beast, the ego, is dead, until *Divine Will* is enthroned as rightful sovereign.

When the human ego has been fully sublimated into the Divine Ego, called Sahaja Samadhi, sadhakas are purified of all vasanas, past habit influences, and the sense of dual wills is no longer present. The fresh spring waters of *Divine Will* then continuously feed the Atman-Soul. Like the thieves on either side of the Christ, the legs are broken of self-will and the sacred *Self-Will* of God reigns free, without a second. Sadhakas then fully realize the three natures of God's Will: **Sat,** the Eternal Self (God the Father), **Chid,** conscious awareness (The Witness, the Son of God), and **Ananda,** bliss that flows as joy in all creation (Divine Mother). All in All is seen as a Divine expression of the Universal Will of God, eternally springing from Joy!

Balanced Sadhana

Balance is a beautiful and delicate word: delicate, and yet enduring from ancient times. The Buddha, when yet performing severe austerities, heard the words of a musician instructing his chela. The musician said, "The strings of this instrument, overly tightened will break, and too loose produce no sound."

Those words changed the Buddha's life and helped him formulate the "middle path."

Once in meditation, a simile made itself known to me. The balance needed on the spiritual path is like the skill needed to sail a boat. The sails must be adjusted just right to get the best speed. Let the sails billow too much and there is a loss of speed, made too taut, again loss of speed. Constant adjustments to the wind and water must be made. The course must be set and kept in line with the rudder and the depth and weight of the keel are essential to keeping the boat upright.

Just so with the spiritual aspirant, the proper tension must be maintained in one's spiritual practice. Too little effort, little progress. Too tense, again, little progress. And the conditions are always changing, so no one rule always applies. The course too must be set. The captain sometimes sails according to the polestar to keep on track. He goes according to the maps and logs left by those who have gone before. So too the sailor on the sea of consciousness: the sadhaka goes according to the Guru, that one who has sailed those seas to his or her ultimate port. Sound reason and intuition of the Divine is the rudder, deepened spiritual practice is the keel. When all is kept in balance, ever-new joy and intuitive soul knowledge become the hallmarks of progress.

In Japan, a craftsman was in apprenticeship for twenty-eight years! Can you imagine, twenty-eight years as the apprentice? Think of the care, the diligence, the patience, and attention to detail that must be required for that apprentice, and the master! The master craftsman may do his or her craft with speed and proficiency. The novice can have one or the other, not both. The tension produced by the master may look effortless to those who don't know, but would break the novice.

It has often been said that the spiritual path is *the* most difficult undertaking known to humankind. How much more so, then, must we take a balanced, proper approach. This balanced approach comes about by creating **pure intention, commitment, loyalty, and an intensity that defies human expectation.**

And, what may we expect in return? Birth into a realized state of Being, to become awakened to, and ultimately one with, the Divinity latent within us all!

> To reach the port of heaven we must sail sometimes with
> the wind and sometimes against it—but we must sail,
> and not drift nor lie at anchor.

> —OLIVER WENDELL HOLMES (1841–1935)

Intention

From the beginning, every conscious being practices **intention,** whether it is choosing food, a mate, clothes, starting a career, or setting the goals of a government. But many people live their lives led by unconscious motivations. The work they do came about because family members or friends got them started in that direction. They had children because their friends were starting families. Guided by social norms, they work, live, dress, and talk as their peers. There is nothing inherently wrong in this, but it does limit a soul's expression only to what is accepted by the crowd.

At some point, the soul yearns to be more conscious of its deeper self and to express it outwardly. The requirement for this deeper expression of the self is breaking out of societal norms and becoming consciously intentional. This produces clarity of who we are beyond social norms and speaks directly to who we wish to be. Immature souls define this as becoming counter-culture. But that merely defines us as, "I am not that!" We then join a group with those who are also counter-culture, then an even *stricter* code of behavior is formed regarding the mode of dress and language.

To know who we are spiritually and to create pure intention from that deep sense of knowing requires courage, effort, and self-awareness. The most efficient way to do this is through quieting the mind in deep prayer and meditation. Gradually, an inner life emerges from the burnt ashes of old patterns. This inner life produces a clarity that prompts us to action. These actions emanate from the clear soul-springs of intuitional knowledge. These emanations are in harmony with those eternal Truths that saints and mystics have enunciated with one voice throughout time.[7] This is the product of pure intention.

When prompted to action through this inner knowing, we become clear on the object of action. With a calm mind, we enact the inner prompting. It may come to us as a complete picture of

---

7   These truths are not harmonious because of some need for conformity; rather, it is because they are universally true.

what is to be, or it may be a step in faith where we know only the next step and no more. In any case, we seek to harmonize the outer action with the inner knowing. The same vibrational pattern we feel inside is put into the outer manifestation.

Pure Intention requires being consciously mindful of each step we take. No detail or aspect is beneath our awareness. When this flow has been fully activated, we feel as if the Divine Presence Itself is acting through us. We realize the reality of pure intention as out-lined in *The Lord's Prayer:* "Thy kingdom come, Thy will be done, on earth as it is in heaven." (Matthew 6:10) The fulfillment of this prayer comes about when we have harmonized our thoughts, words, and actions with the highest intuitional wisdom of the soul.

God the Architect

Who Thou art I know not,
But this much I know:
Thou has set the Pleiades
In a silver row;

Thou has sent the trackless winds
Loose upon their way;
Thou hast reared a colored wall
Twixt the night and day;

Thou hast made the flowers to bloom
And the stars to shine;
Hid rare gems of richest ore
In the tunneled mine—

But chief of all Thy wondrous works,
Supreme of all thy plan,
Thou hast put an upward reach
Into the heart of Man.

—HARRY KEMP (1883–1960)

Commitment

Now, to realize the enactment of pure intention requires **commitment.** Once we decide to move in a certain direction, we bring all the forces we have available to bear to make it manifest. Whenever we make the choice for one action, we rule out 99.9% of the other possible actions. If I choose to live in Seattle, Washington, I will be excluding every other city in the world to live in at this time. Rather than be preoccupied with the idea of living somewhere else, better to be fully focused on where I am now.

The same is true with a moment in time. I can daydream all day of a time in the past or time yet to be, but what a difference when I practice being present to this moment. These may sound like self-evident statements, but most people are not fully present in the here and now! So, commitment means to be fully present to our choice in this moment. And, it means to bring our full sense of being into the fray.

I remember a time when I really became aware that "This is *my* life," and it was up to me to live it! This is my time on the stage and if I do not fully commit myself to it, I will be the same as the player on a sports team who is seated in the spectators' bleachers during the game, wondering why the game is not going well! Our time here is limited and if we do not choose to fully live now, then when? Full-hearted commitment means to take our life seriously and make it count.

> Dare Greatly —
> It is not the critic who counts; not the man who points out how the strong man stumbled or where the doer of deeds could have done better. The credit belongs to the man who is actually in the arena; whose face is marred by dust and sweat and blood; who strives valiantly, who errs and comes short again and again; who knows the great enthusiasms, the great devotions, and spends himself in a worthy cause; who at the best knows the

triumph of high achievement; and who at the worst, if he fails, at least fails while daring greatly; so that his place shall never be with those cold and timid souls who know neither victory nor defeat.

—Theodore Roosevelt (1858–1919)

Loyalty

In order for our commitment to count, we need to cultivate **loyalty**. There are those who are sparked by an idea, commit themselves to it, then fade before the finish line. Like the gold diggers who shovel their way down five feet into the ground in search of the treasure, only to start a second dig that penetrates the ground ten feet. Again and again, they begin new holes. All the while, the mother lode is at a twenty-foot depth! Never loyally committing themselves to dig to twenty feet at any one place, they dig countless other holes that add up to hundreds of feet in depth. In defeat, they cry, "There's no gold in them thar hills!"

When we find a path to God-consciousness we have faith in, we should stay with it until we reach our destination. Practicing loyalty in friendship, work, marriage, and parenting is all part of building a pattern in our life. This does not mean going along with something that feels absolutely wrong out of so-called loyalty. Short of that, loyalty will build our character and will get us over those little and big bumps that inevitably occur in any commitment.

When I was traveling in India, a western woman asked if I would teach her a higher Kriya technique. She said, "I have a teacher here in India, but he won't give the higher initiation. Indian time and my time are just different." She was telling me right there and then why she wasn't ready for higher initiation! Loyalty should not be given lightly, nor should it be withdrawn easily. In previous generations, "A man was as good as his word." And, if he shook hands on a deal, he was loyal to his commitment. The world suffers today from broken agreements and disloyalty. The practice of loyalty, too, makes for good relationships, good business, good government, and a healthy society. And finally, loyalty is a key to all spiritual progress.

> The kingdom of God is a society of the best men, working for the best ends, according to the best methods. Its law is one word—loyalty.

> —HENRY DRUMMOND (1851–1897)

Desire That Defies all Human Expectation

> Great minds have purposes, others have wishes.
> Little minds are tamed and subdued by misfortune;
> but great minds rise above them.

> —WASHINGTON IRVING (1783–1859)

Great, high-minded goals always come at a cost; oftentimes the greater the goal, the higher the cost. In spiritual transformation, the cost is the life of the ego, which is identification with the body. Since the ego is who we have come to think of ourselves to be, it translates into a willingness to give our ego to God. Naturally, this would require a **desire that defies all human expectation**. Human expectation will do much for the anticipation of wealth, fame, security, or pleasure. All of these are thrown into the fires of renunciation! So human expectation cannot play a part in this journey. And what about desire?

What explorer, scientist, inventor, or anyone with a worthy goal became successful without the intensity of desire? How much more so then for the spiritual scientist/explorer. Krishna says that out of many thousands there is one, here and there, who seeks out realization in a real way. (Gita 7:3) And, out of those rare seekers, one here or there becomes fully realized. Why? Is it because of a capricious god who whimsically grants this one entry and not others? No! Humankind is born with free will. No one else determines our direction in life.

We choose! We choose to get up in the morning and meditate or roll over and go back to sleep. We choose to keep our mind on God in service during the day or identify with ego desires and attachments. We choose! And in that choosing, we determine the course of our life.

If we find lukewarm desire for realization, or any worthy goal, then we must pray deeply for greater intensity, and *not* to stop that prayer until we get what we need! We are born with potential in the ready, but we must make ourselves receptive. Divine Grace is always in and around us like a boundless sea. Prayer is not to make a god of a fickle mind—it is to change us! In some distant past, we closed and locked the doors to Grace. Only one person is in charge of changing that condition. We must exercise the same intensity in opening our own closed and locked door to God's Grace as we expended in closing it in the first place.

> Our duty to God is to make ourselves the most perfect
> product of divine incarnation that we can become. This
> is possible only through the pursuit of worthy ideals.
>
> —EDGAR WHITE BURRILL (1883–1958)

How many times does another New Year's celebration find us repeating halfhearted resolutions for the next? Let us create great desire to open the door to Grace and supercharge our will with Divine Will! United with Divine Will and surrendering ourselves to it, we become spiritually balanced. We weigh the anchor of indifference and set sail at best speed to our Heavenly Goal. In order to make the goal of Self-realization, and all worthy goals, cultivate today pure intention, commitment, loyalty, and that intensity that defies all human expectation.

John the Baptist proclaimed the kingdom of heaven is here, now! (Matthew 3:2) Jesus echoed that and boldly taught that God and the kingdom of heaven are within you. (Luke 17:21) It always has been. Their voices call to us from down through the ages in concert with realized Beings from every part of the world and from every age. The time is now! The place here! And, if we proceed on the balanced middle path, with high-mindedness, we will discover gold, not of the cold ground, but of the all-embracing, never-ending Spirit. May that realization be yours *now* and *always.*

Awaken O Divine Mother

O Divine Mother
In purity, You have inwardly called me to Yourself.
But also, in outer beguiling forms
You come to tempt me away.

You are the sacred Power within
And secretly You yearn to rise
Through subtle channels that flow,
To awaken Divine experience itself!

But age-old patterns strive to divert
That steady minded approach
And seek to worship lesser gods
In vain pursuit of carnal happiness.

Awaken in me, O Divine Mother,
Pure love for Thy Divine Form alone.
Burn those puny tempting idols in fiery sacred flame,
And free me, now and always, in Thee alone!

God: With and Without Form

I s there only one God? The answer is, unequivocally, yes! "Hear O Israel, the Lord our God, the Lord is one." (Deuteronomy 6:4) God, being omnipotent (all-powerful), omniscient (all-knowing), and omnipresent (everywhere present), is the only force and intelligence there is. Therefore, God really is one, without a second.

Now, how to explain multiplicity, which is God appearing as the separate forces, beings, and perspectives that we see in all creation around us. In India, the yogis have a concept called Maya. Maya is God creating an apparent separation where none truly exists. In deep sleep, we unconsciously experience ourselves to be one with God; all separation ceases to exist. To consciously be in that state (which yogis call samadhi) we would know ever-new bliss, be fully conscious, and know ourselves to be ever existent.

However, that conscious awareness is rare amongst most of humankind. The veil of Maya keeps us separate from this knowledge. Nevertheless, realized Beings, from ancient times to modern, have attested to its veracity through their direct experience. The history of religion is also the history of the evolution of consciousness. Early humans, intimately acquainted with nature, worshipped the spirits that live in and control those elements. As humankind evolved from hunter-gatherers to agrarian, the power of the sun, seasons, and celestial movements took on greater meaning and resulted in the worship of God in those forms. Gradually, as we know from recorded history, the development of higher consciousness occurred. Mystics began to experience deeper insights into what we call God. Transcendent visions revealed more refined states of Being beyond this physical reality.

Spiritual scientists, exploring the laboratory of their own consciousness, came to understand this singular Reality called God. The names and rituals regarding this understanding of God's nature vary throughout the world, according to language and cultural differences. But the principles remain unchanged as to the nature of God and the seemingly ephemeral nature of this physical reality. Ancient records reveal the earliest affirmations of this central truth coming from the East in India and in the West, with Judaism. A monotheism evolved in India that recognized a unified field of consciousness that permeates all creation yet stands beyond that which is created. Through careful mapping of consciousness, a new inner cosmology appeared. In Judaism, a singular creative cause was revealed to its early seers, and came to be known as: **I Am That I Am.**

These two impersonal concepts of a universal Divinity, one from India, one from The Middle East, moved theology forward in our recorded history. This was not, and has not been, a smooth progression. Resistive forces of tribalism, privileged classism, unwarranted dogmatism, divisive sectarianism, corruption, and the influence of lesser minds took their toll on these truths. No religion and no area of the world were left unscathed during these past dark ages.

Saints and realized Beings have stood as spiritual bulwarks to keep alive the true spirit of religion. Transcending institutions and privileged classes, these brave souls were often persecuted in their own times. But the sweetness and purity of their lives and the truths they taught spoke to those in need of spiritual example and upliftment. Spiritual Truth, like all universal principles, transcends the small-minded and vindictive. Although Spiritual Truth has been crucified innumerable times in millions of hearts, still the Light finds fertile soil in those who are yearning and receptive. Some religions banned the worship and veneration of saints or symbolic deities. Often, the practices of worship of these deities were crude throwbacks to earlier developmental stages in religion. These forms of worship were discouraged, many times with the sharp edge of a sword. Impassioned believers came to see the worship of a deity as an affront to God.

In other religions such as in India, these symbolic deities were seen as so many expressions of the monotheistic Supreme Being. Recognizing a human need to focus on images, saints, and deities, this form of worship was fostered as a legitimate avenue of approach to a singular Divinity. Stories of these saints and deities are charming, emotionally engaging, and instructive. Passionate prayers, songs, and rituals evince a lasting value to these expressions of Divinity. There has, however, been much quarreling over the matter of what is appropriate worship of God. Is worship of forms in keeping with the highest truth?

Moses first knew God through direct perception as a voice in a burning bush. Later, he built a simple stone altar to worship God. When the people of Israel reinstituted an older worship of Baal, the response was swift and severe. It was at that time Moses gave instructions for the creation of an elaborate temple that was made of gold, silver, and cloth of purple and lavender. An ark was created that depicted twin seraphim and a priestly class was formed to conduct rites of worship, including animal sacrifice. The people had an object on which to focus their attention.

Christians have no representation of God the Father, but the crucified Son of Man is in the front of most churches, or at least a cross; there are pictures of Jesus in homes, and Catholics use pictures of Mother Mary and the saints. Islam prohibits any human depictions of saints or of God, but those of Islamic faith have put their creative talents into the architecture and construction of the mosque. And, although the Buddha forbade the use of images, I doubt if any image has been more reproduced than the Buddha's!

We can see through these examples that the human mind, in many cases, needs objects of adoration and worship. Finding it difficult to focus the mind and devotion on a God who is beyond form, beginningless and endless, devotees are very often attracted to holy places and personages to whom they can relate. Again, is this in keeping with the highest truth?

In the Bhagavad Gita, Krishna holds out the Universal Vision[8] as the supreme attainment. He, speaking from that Universal Consciousness, says that those who worship God's lower forms

---

8   Universal Vision: the realization of God as the Supreme Being manifest as all creation and beyond creation as formless, beginningless, and endless spirit.

sincerely, He accepts that worship as well. (Gita 9:23) The true essence is the purity of heart in worship. That is, loving God for God alone and not for what we can get from our worship in terms of material success, power over people, or nature. This expresses my conviction also. I think most of us need a focus for our attention and for inspiration. In order to progress more quickly to the Universal Vision, however, we should always affirm that the Light we behold in the visage of a realized master or deity is a manifestation of the Universal Divine Light. As a stained-glass window cannot illumine itself, so no spiritual master or deity can be anything but a conduit of God. Constantly bring to mind the Universal Light in what we are worshiping in form. Let us pierce the outer form of the image and go straight to the inner source of our adoration.

If our mind is focused on an individual aspect of God, then practice seeing that aspect in all people and all creation. If our chosen ideal is Jesus or Krishna, then practice seeing Jesus or Krishna in the hearts of everyone we meet. Many years ago, I was blessed with the experience of seeing Mother's face in the heart center of every person I met. For twenty-four hours, I was in this experience and all the walls of separation crumbled between others and myself. This was my first glimpse that God resides in the heart of all people, each one a shrine of the omnipresent Spirit.

From the beginning, my attention was drawn to that indwelling formless Presence of God. The one universal principle in religion is the path of the spine and the brain. Through my focus on the ajna and feeling the Presence in my spine and brain, the transformation of body, mind, and soul continued. Over time, the spiritual masters revealed to me their unique signature of Light that is at once personal and impersonal. Now I hang their images on the wall to remind me of their sweet presence and protection. All who enter my home also have this uplifting influence.

Mother was very focused on her own Guru, and that focus took her all the way to the feet of God. As a final gesture, she even threw that into the ocean of God Consciousness. Later, when she set her altar, it was with the simplicity of flowers, candles, and some incense. She did not display pictures, although she had a large picture of her Guru, Sri Yoganandaji, on the wall opposite her chair in her home. Every fully realized master has overcome all limiting forms of worship, but many continue on with veneration for God in certain forms as an example to those who follow after them or for their own purposes. Worship of God with form or without form is all due to personal preference. Ultimately, all worship should take us to the Universal Vision: the realization that God is nirguna, formless spirit, and saguna, with form, having taken form ultimately as all creation. The Vision of God as both formless and with form is the highest realization.

There is a fascinating account of two highly realized souls regarding this subject. Ramakrishna Paramhansa was living at Dakshineswar, a temple compound near Calcutta. Ramakrishna worshipped God in the form of Kali, the Divine Mother. One day a wandering monk, Totapuri, came to Dakshineswar and recognized Ramakrishna's great spirit and decided to initiate him into Vedanta. Vedanta holds that the world is an illusion and God is only to be found in transcendent Spirit. Here I will give a brief account of Totapuri's initiation of Ramakrishna.[9]

> Totapuri began to impart to Ramakrishna the great truths of Vedanta. "Brahman," he said, is the only Reality, ever pure, ever illumined, ever free, beyond the limits of time, space, and causation. Though apparently divided by names and forms through the inscrutable power of maya, that enchantress who makes the impossible possible, Brahman is really one and undivided. When a seeker merges in the beatitude of samadhi, the seeker does not perceive time and space or name and form, the offspring of maya. Whatever is within the domain of maya is unreal. Give it up. Destroy the prison-house of name and form and rush out of it with the strength of a

---

9   *The Gospel of Sri Ramakrishna* (pp. 28–31).

lion. Dive deep in search of the Self and realize It through samadhi. You will find the world of name and form vanishing into the void, and the puny ego dissolving in Brahman-consciousness. You will realize your identity with Brahman, Existence-Knowledge-Bliss Absolute.

… Totapuri asked the disciple to withdraw his mind from all objects of the relative world, including the gods and goddesses, and to concentrate on the Absolute. But the task was not easy even for Sri Ramakrishna. He found it impossible to take his mind beyond Kali, the Divine Mother of the Universe. "After the initiation," Ramakrishna once said, describing the event, "Nangta began to teach me the various conclusions of the Advaita (God without form or attributes) Vedanta and asked me to withdraw the mind completely from all objects and dive deep into the Atman. But in spite of all my attempts, I could not altogether cross the realm of name and form and bring my mind to the unconditioned state. I had no difficulty taking the mind from all the objects of the world. But the radiant and too familiar figure of the Blissful Mother, the embodiment of the essence of Pure Consciousness, appeared before me as a living reality. Her bewitching smile prevented me from passing into the great beyond. Again and again, I tried, but She stood in my way every time. In despair, I turned to Nangta: 'It is hopeless. I cannot raise my mind to the unconditioned state and come face to face with Atman.' He grew excited and sharply said: 'What? You cannot do it? But you have to!' He cast his eyes around. Finding a piece of glass, he took it up and struck it between my eyebrows. 'Concentrate the mind on this point!' he thundered. Then with a stern determination, I again sat to meditate. As soon as the gracious form of the Divine Mother appeared before me, I used my discrimination as a sword and with it clove Her in two. The last barrier fell. My spirit at once soared beyond the relative plane and I lost myself in samadhi."

Sri Ramakrishna remained completely absorbed in samadhi for three days. "Is this really true?" Totapuri cried in astonishment. "Is it possible that he has attained in a single day what it took me forty years of strenuous practice to achieve? Great God! It is nothing short of a miracle." With the help of Totapuri, Sri Ramakrishna's mind finally came down to the relative plane.

Totapuri, a monk of the most orthodox type, never stayed at a place more than three days. But he remained at Dakshineswar for eleven months. He too had something to learn.... He ridiculed the spending of emotion on the worship of a personal God.... About this time, Totapuri was suddenly laid up with a severe attack of dysentery. On account of this miserable illness, he found it impossible to meditate. One night, the pain became excruciating. He could no longer concentrate on Brahman. The body stood in the way. He became incensed with its demands. A free soul, he did not at all care for the body. So, he determined to drown it in the Ganges. Thereupon he walked into the river. But, lo! He walks to the other bank. Is there not enough water in the Ganges? Standing dumbfounded on the other bank he looks back across the water. The trees, the temples, the houses, are silhouetted against the sky. Suddenly, in one dazzling moment, he sees on all sides the presence of the Divine Mother. She is in everything; She is everything. She is the mind. She is pain. She is death. She is everything that one sees, hears, or imagines. She turns "yea" into "nay," and "nay" into "yea." Without Her grace, no embodied being can go beyond Her realm.... She resides in Her Transcendental, Absolute aspect. She is the Brahman that Totapuri had been worshipping all his life. Totapuri returned to Dakshineswar and spent the remaining hours of the night meditating on the Divine Mother. In the morning he went to the Kali temple with Sri Ramakrishna and prostrated himself before the image of the Mother.

God, being both with form and formless, is both personal and impersonal. His Form is filled with the formless. The formless Spirit always has form.[10] One cannot separate the one from the other. The potential problem for a sadhaka comes when there is an attachment to form that precludes them from gaining the Universal Vision. In India, they say a thorn in the foot, deeply embedded, can be removed by using another thorn. That is, to transcend the realm of limiting thoughts, we can use a thought, a mantra, or an image of God, in order to ascend to overarching Spirit. With that transcendence, we come face to face with the Universal Consciousness and come to realize that all is God, One without a second. Placing the attention on God, with or without form, seek out His very real Presence, and let Him usher us into His Universal Vision.

---

10   Sri Yukteswar's delightful description from the *Autobiography of a Yogi* (pp. 404–5): "Joyous astral festivities on the higher astral planets like Hiranyaloka take place when a being is liberated from the astral world through spiritual advancement and is, therefore, ready to enter the heaven of the causal world. On such occasions, the Invisible Heavenly Father, and the saints who are merged in Him, materialize themselves into bodies of their own choice and join the astral celebration. In order to please His beloved devotee, the Lord takes any desired form. If the devotee worshipped through devotion, he sees God as the Divine Mother. To Jesus, the Father-aspect of the Infinite One was appealing beyond other conceptions. The individuality with which the Creator has endowed each of His creatures makes every conceivable and inconceivable demand on the Lord's versatility!"

Gardening with God

Three Gunas, or qualities, associate themselves with human life.

The first quality is sattva. Sattvic qualities are those attuned to the spiritual, such as search for truth, devotion, selfless service, a loving nature, meditation, and other spiritual practices. These lead to a refined personality that is saintly in nature.

The second Guna is rajas. Rajasic qualities are activating, stimulating of desire for the things of the world. Desire for name, fame, fortune, dominance, and emotions such as anger all result from the rajasic nature. It tends to be restless, always on the move.

The third Guna is tamas. Tamasic qualities are depressive in nature, drawing our mind into smaller spheres of awareness. Examples of tamasic qualities are: depression, jealousy, fear of loss, and pettiness. These can lead to a degradation of the personality, even to the point of suicide.

Much of life in the world today is a play between the forces of tamas and rajas, with a little sattva. Of course, for the sadhaka to progress spiritually, cultivation of a sattvic nature is the goal. But when we as sadhakas are confronted with habits, stemming from past actions of the rajasic and tamasic natures, what do we do?

One method is to graft the rajasic or tamasic desire or habit onto a sattvic root. To do this, we change the root cause assumption behind the drive of a lower nature. For instance, if we have a strong drive for worldly success, which is quite appropriate at certain times in life, Sadhakas still want to have the right relationship with that drive rather than have it carry them off to even more worldly desires and attachment. So, the sadhaka changes his or her mind-set about that drive for worldly success by seeing it as God who is expressing Himself in that desire through the mind of the sadhaka. In other words, it is God who desires success in the world. By constantly bringing to mind the root association of God, the prior ego association of, "This is my desire," is lessened and finally becomes resolved in the new thought.

An example would be a rajasic desire for name, fame, and fortune as an entertainer. It feels to the sadhaka that his or her entire world revolves around that one desire, even though he or she has been given the desire for Self-realization as well. By constantly thinking, "This is God who desires to be a successful entertainer," the relationship of the self to the desire changes. Gradually the sadhaka becomes a third person watching God moving through the outward personality as the entertainer. With this third-person perspective, attachment to results lessen, as the results are surrendered to God. An inner calm begins to emanate from a deep place within, moving the sadhaka from restless rajasic nature to an inwardly calm sattvic nature. An additional advantage to the sattvic nature is that the calm mind's acuity for observation is heightened, critical for any art, craft, or intellectual pursuit.

Beyond these boons in performance, the tamasic natures of depression and jealousy are eliminated, sadhakas can become more balanced, more professional, and less prone to excesses such as drug and sex addictions.

This grafting technique can also be used with tamasic nature as well. For instance, we may tend toward depression, sadness, despondency, feelings of hopelessness and helplessness, etc. The way to graft those qualities onto God is to associate all those thoughts and feelings to God Himself. The feeling of sadness and loss is the feeling of sadness and loss at having lost connection with God, the source of all Joy and Love. In the past, those feelings were connected with the loss of a person, place, or situation that is no longer in the sadhakas' life. Any or all of those connections are switched to one category: inner loss of connection with God. By the constant new association of grafting this feeling to God, we open our heart to the healing Light that can come only from God. This opening to the Light adds sweetness to our sorrow and eventually changes it to a mood of Joy and a Love stemming from the new internal root association with Spirit.

The idea of helplessness gets grafted on to the new root by mentally knowing that the ego is helpless to give true happiness. Only by surrendering the idea, "I am the doer," and admitting the ego is help-less, do we connect with the real source of power that is God. With that connection comes the realization that Grace is the real power of accomplishment and regeneration. In that recognition, the power of Grace begins to transform sadhakas into something new, something sattvic in nature.

Any quality not of sattvic nature can be grafted in this way. What about sexual desire? Sexual desire is the desire for union, oneness, which is turned outward; that is, finding one's counterpart in the world. By affirming the intense desire for union by grafting it onto desire for Cosmic Consciousness, we utilize that powerful energy for upward propulsion into sacred realms. It is in this Cosmic Consciousness the desire for union is truly fulfilled, versus a relentless search on the out-side punctuated by occasional fulfillment.

By this positive grafting approach, we actually utilize the energy of the desire by giving it a new rootstock. This is far superior to surrounding ourselves with the negations, "Not this, not that, can I do." A concern may come, "Won't this focus on a desire increase that desire rather than change it?" If we do it properly, the results will let us know we are on the right track. Confirmation will come by increased calm, inner joy, and a love that comes spontaneously from the heart. We will find ourselves less attached to the out-comes and get joy in the sheer doing of the activity itself. And, if the activity is not suitable to sattvic energy, it will lose its attraction for the sadhaka. Like oil on water, the two will not mix. In these ways we can judge for ourselves our progress.

Cultivating sattvic qualities will necessitate letting go of some old activities. But the inner joy that comes as a result of attune-ment to our good, will more than fulfill the empty promises of out-ward enjoyment of wrong activity. A feeling of inner purity will rise up within sadhakas that no worldly gain can duplicate. Expansion of Spirit-awareness and a renewed sense of who and what the sad-haka really is will be the growth, blooming, and fruition of a life rooted in sattvic nature.

Brahmacharya

The word brahmacharya is a Hindu word denoting celibacy. In the Vedas, the ancient sacred writings of India, four stages of life are laid out.

The first twenty-five years are categorized as the student phase, or being a brahmachari (brahmacharini, feminine). Traditionally, youths (male) left home when they became eight years or older. They lived at a hermitage or with a teacher. Here, they were taught how to live a spiritual life and received an education in reading, writing, math, astronomy, etc. During this time, they remained celibate and were often taught by teachers who also observed celibacy. Most then moved to the second stage of life, that of the householder. A very few, who felt called, would continue as celibates, but this was rare. It was during the time of Adi Shankaracharya, who became a renunciant at a young age and reorganized the order of swamis, that becoming a renunciant while still young became more widely practiced in Hindu culture.

When we take a survey of religious traditions around the world, we find celibacy, abstaining from sex, is observed in all major traditions in one form or another in regard to living a spiritual life. Why? The inward reason has to do with physiology, psychology, and spirituality.

The physiology of the body and the pranology[11] of the astral body reveal the true nature of sexual energy and sublimation. Sublimation comes from the Latin root *sublima*, which means to elevate. Its Webster's definition is: "Psychology: to divert the energy of (a sexual or other biological impulse) from its immediate goal to one of a higher social, moral, or aesthetic nature or use." It is well known that artists and intellectuals, when consumed with their chosen field, will oftentimes be abstinent. Far from feeling this is a sacrifice, they know the inward pleasure of transformed energy.

---

11   Pranology: the study of prana or life-force.

What Webster's definition leaves out is the spiritual element, not yet understood in most of Western thought.

In India and other cultures of the East, it has been long understood that the transformation of sexual energy, called kundalini, is essential for Spiritual Realization. Yoga calls life-energy "prana." Prana is the essential stuff that allows us to move, think, and operate in this body. It is the indefinable "something" that leaves the body at the time of death, along with consciousness. It is intelligent, yet is responsive to individual will. It is primarily of the astral body, too fine an energy for human detection on a physical realm, but nevertheless can be experienced, and is experienced by all. This energy carries on the building and maintenance of the body. Good health is dependent on its balanced functioning. It should not be too surprising this energy has not yet been discovered by Western science. Since it is not detectable by instruments, it remains hidden. How many laws of nature do we take for granted now, but at one time were unseen by uncomprehending minds of science? Yogic science tells us there is coiled-up potential life-force at the base of the spine that is normally dormant. Under certain circumstances, this energy in potential can be released and becomes a transformative force for evolution of the consciousness. When this occurs the condensed life-force at the base of the spine streams up the astral spine into higher regions of the consciousness. It is here that the real work of the kundalini takes place. These higher centers of awareness are activated, changed from their previously dormant status to being active and alive with energy and awareness. This leads to the gradual ascendancy of consciousness to becoming fully awakened, or illumined. For such a one, the titles of Christ or Buddha may be rightfully applied.

The psychological aspects of this awakening concern the changes the mind goes through in this unfoldment. In order for complete awakening to occur, a total change in thought process is required. Yoga science has two categories for normal mental functioning for human beings. The first is manas. Manas may be thought of as the more developmentally primitive part of the mind. The second category is the Buddhi. The Buddhi is the higher realm of reasoning that is said to be unique to humans. Through abstractions, humans may philosophize, create more complex tools, etc. This is the power of Buddhi when focused on human endeavors. When the Buddhi is spiritualized, it has the capacity to perceive spiritual consciousness.

When the transformative energy of the kundalini is activated, a battle ensues over the domination of the human psyche. The manas traits of the animal mind and the Buddhi-intellect, focused on human endeavors, carry on with the momentum gained over many lifetimes. This lower mind of the human lies in direct contradiction to the spontaneous flow of Divine consciousness ever streaming to the sensitive brain when it has been awakened. The psychological and physiological battle that ensues is the stuff of which so many scriptures and myths concern themselves.

In this way, we see tremendous changes occurring on the physiological, pranalogical, and psychological levels of existence. If the sadhaka feels besieged at times, this is a ready reason why! Understanding all three levels of this battle will help illustrate the power of sublimation, so closely akin to the word sublime.

Sexuality has often been associated with the fall of man. When we look at the physiology of humans, it is obvious in design that human beings were meant to be sexual in nature. Why then the emphasis on sex as the apple of temptation? If you imagine a person's nervous system running from the base of the spine to the top of the head, and in that image, think of the brain as the roots of the tree, turned upside down, then the trunk of the tree is the spine, running down the back of the torso to the tailbone. All of the afferent and efferent nerves running to and from are the branches of this nervous system tree. Each branch of this tree represents some sensory experience in the body. Each of the sensory experiences calls for the attention of the brain. All these nerve centers operate simultaneously, each with their own messages for the center of experience, the brain.

What we know from oriental pranalogy of the subtle astral body, with its seventy-two thousand nadis (astral nerves), reveals powerhouses all along the spine and brain. The three powerhouses located toward the base of the spine control functions of the body and human will as they operate in the world. The chakra power-houses from the heart up to the top of the head, are mostly sleeping. Humans, in their full capacity, have those upper regions awakened. The highest region is at the top of the head, called the Sahasrara, and when this center is fully awakened—illumined—the knowledge of our oneness with the omniscient, omnipresent, omnipotent Spiritual Consciousness becomes a fact. What this means for the potential evolution of consciousness cannot be overstated. This awakening is the real purpose behind religion and all great philosophies.

As we imagine this upside-down tree, with all of its fruits of experiences, seeing, hearing, touching, smelling, tasting, we can easily see how our attention is drawn to these captivating sensations. What about those higher centers, why don't we know more about them? The myths of all the great religions depict "the fall of man," or the entry of humanity into a delusive nature. This is always associated somehow with the body, and usually has something to do with sex consciousness. Physiologically the sex organs reside at the most distant point from the roots of this tree of consciousness, the Sahasrara, or the crown of the head. Pranalogically the sex organs represent a great magnetic pull away from the higher centers of consciousness. Psychologically, the sex urge focuses the attention for union on oneness away from an interior union of Spirit toward finding a complementary soul "out there." Symbolically and functionally, sex energy and sex consciousness represent the furthest extreme from oneness in Spiritual Consciousness.

A revelation showed me the inner meaning of the Adam and Eve story when the serpent was "sentenced" by God to crawl upon its belly. This is symbolic language for a natural cause-and-effect consequence of entering into this mundane world of experience at the expense of our fully awakened Spiritual Nature. The serpent is the kundalini force, designed to feed the upper regions of consciousness with life-force. When consciousness is directed by the will to flow to the exterior world, and most powerfully through the sexual organs (the fruit in the midst of the garden), to the exclusion of the higher centers of consciousness, the vast kundalini power becomes mostly dormant. There is sufficient life-force to enliven the lower centers of consciousness; nothing more is being utilized. The more highly charged energy of the kundalini would prove harmful to the soul focused on the outer events of the world alone. So, the serpent, the kundalini, crawls upon its belly, or remains dormant below the belly button within the spine.

The kundalini and the higher regions of consciousness wait for their awakening. In order for this awakening to occur, the redirection of the will from outer worldly consciousness, with its all-consuming attraction, to the inner world of Spirit is needed. As long as the attention is focused purely on the sensory world and its preoccupations, so long will the inner nature of Spiritual Consciousness remain dormant. Brahmacharya is not simply abstaining from sex. Brahma is the Self, or God in Its absolute form. Achari means he or she who lives in—so, a Brahmachari is one who lives within the Self, or is God-realized. By transmuting the life-energy that is normally spent on worldly pursuits, raising it up the spine, and activating the higher centers of consciousness, we advance spiritually. When the kundalini, the coiled-up life-energy at the base of the spine, becomes activated, then the whole spinal system becomes charged, electrified with this dynamic evolutionary force. This is the fuel for the awakening, to become a Buddha.

For the sadhaka on the path, this upward ascent is the goal of the aspirant. But is it necessary for the sadhaka to abstain from all sexual activity? There is a time in the sadhana of an aspirant when all the forces, both human and divine, are focused on this upward journey. For the sadhaka, there may be a variety of circumstances in which they find themselves leading a brahmacharya life. A devotee may be unmarried; a couple may choose to be leading a celibate life while married, or circumstances may result in abstinence beyond the control of a married couple. Mother taught that to lead a normal sexual life as a married couple was the best for the vast majority of aspirants. It is better to experience the fullness of marital love and know what it can offer and what it does not offer in order for the aspirant to see it clearly for what it is. Mother often said that the love shared between the married couple in the sexual act represented the highest experience on the human level. This is especially true when the relationship is spiritualized. Mother described a time in her own marriage when all desire for sex dropped off. With this spontaneous dropping off of sexual desire in her own ascent to the Divine, she held out as a model for married couples. No doubt this is a sensitive subject when this dropping off happens for one of the partners and not for the other. However, if love and caring are present, all such difficulties can be managed. Eventually, for all, the time will come for the complete focus to be on God alone.

We who have not been acquainted with the potential that can result from this interior union may eye celibacy with some suspicion. The focus of our mind may be trained on what is being given up, versus what is being gained. We have been so conditioned, especially in modern Western culture, to think of sex as the "be all, end all" of human experience. Without the idea of the transmutation of the energy and the awakening of these higher centers, this concept would be all about denying ourselves what comes naturally for no obvious gain. Those who have had some experiences in uplifted consciousness may get a glimpse of what is possible. Others may have an intuitive hunch of its value, and others may have an intellectual grasp of the potential. We are in fact struggling with eons of programming regarding the sexual impulse. Take away the subconscious programming from other lifetimes, and we are still the result, biologically, of thousands of years of sexually driven parentage. It is in our genes to reproduce! To redirect this energy is no joke, and should not be taken as a given to happen so easily, or that if we struggle with it there is something wrong with us. This is a momentous shift of will, and while very possible, it should be thought of soberly, in the light of day.

The process of working our way through material creation as a conscious entity may be thought of, to this point, as evolution. We have been involved with knowing this material creation from the ground up, literally. We have experienced ourselves to be matter of minerals, matter of the livelier vegetable kingdom, matter of the mobile animal kingdom, and finally, matter of the higher reasoning faculty of human beings. From evolution, we now move to involution: the shift from exterior consciousness, the exterior world of the five senses, to the interior world of inner awakening and intuitive Divine perception.

Our long journey into this material world and exile from our spiritual home is coming to a close. When we are ready, we will start this new journey and awaken to this inner reality. For those still focused and intent on the outer reality, there will be incomprehension and disbelief in this inner reality. But what of it? They are satisfied with their current experience. But for those ready to awaken to this world of Light within, nothing else will ultimately do. Thus, we shift our attention from evolution to involution.

The Means of Brahmacharya

The Nature of Sexual Energy and Sublimation

First, recognize that sexual energy within mankind is one of the most powerful forces there is. That is why the human race continues: the miracle of new life is spawned as a result. It is also the reason sex is used to sell so many things, and when it is out of control, why the effects can be so devastating. Next, there is the idea amongst many religious schools that sex is bad, a terrible thing. However, since sex produces babies, one of life's most precious gifts, how can that be bad? Sexuality brings the union of husband and wife closer together in love and intimacy; how can that be bad? It is not the use, but the misuse of sexual energy that creates positive or negative conditions. Since it is such a powerful force, its potential for good and bad consequences is also powerful.

Given that it is powerful, and that the life-energy within sexual energy is power itself, you must use wisdom in the expression or transmutation of this energy. To begin the discussion on the means of sublimating sexual energy into spiritual-creative energy, create a positive goal in your mind. Since mind is the beginning of all creative processes, create a picture in your mind of what you would look like as a brahmacharya. As a realized brahmacharya, you have gained full self-mastery of yourself and raised that powerful force into the higher regions of your Being. Begin with looking at yourself as another person would see you in that transformed state. Inwardly, the fuel that comes from sexual energy is streaming up your spine; it has opened the heart, throat, ajna, and crown chakras (the consciousness powerhouses in the higher spine and brain). Although the invisible energy is not seen with the two physical eyes, nevertheless it produces an effect on the physical body and subtle bodies that is perceptible. As that third person looking back on your illumined self, do you see a glow on the face? Do you notice a shine in the eyes? More subtly, do you feel a vibration of peace and love emanating from that one? When that self speaks, do you sense a vibration in the voice that "awakens your better angels?" Take some time to fill in this picture in your mind's eye before reading on.

Now, enter the body of yourself as the realized brahmacharya. What do you notice about the way you stand, the way you carry yourself, the way you breathe? Next, notice the flow of your thoughts, the activation of creative centers, and access to higher consciousness. Now, notice the flow of energy within your body. And now all around your body. Take your time. Breathe into this picture and be careful to notice everything about this state of being. This is your future potential self!

Now observe how the sexual organs operate and life-energy flows into the spine and to these higher centers. In your imagination, as you see these centers fully open, ask yourself, "Am I missing anything essential by using this energy inwardly rather than out-wardly?" If you really follow through on this exercise, you will real-ize that the life of a brahmacharya has its advantages.

I am not intending to sell you on the idea that being a brahmach-arya is the only way to live your life. I am in hopes that you may get an inkling of the richness of the life possible through sublimation, what may have been before, unseen possibilities. You have been so indoctrinated into thinking that sex is the "be all, end all" of human experience, that to consider a life of brahmacharya as fulfilling is a rarity. You can now dispense with outmoded caricatures of the cel-ibate as stilted, prudish, and life-denying. The potential for a life as a brahmacharya is unlimited, fascinating, and open-ended beyond our current imagining.

Moving Into the Life of a Brahmacharya

Self-mastery begins with mastery of your thoughts. Jesus is quoted as saying that to even desire another man's wife is adultery. This is a very strict criterion indeed! But it speaks to the power of thought. Thought is the primal creator of all that is. *When you think, you cre-ate.* That is why I had you paint a picture in your mind of a complete brahmacharya; you may want to do that often, every day, several times a day, and especially as you go to sleep at night and when you first awaken.

When you realize that thought is creation, it begins to dawn on you how important it is when you create intention. Thoughts can be spread all over the place, with little power to create. Or, they can be focused like a laser that can cut through all obstacles to find ful-fillment. **Self-mastery includes the creation of pure intention; that is, those focused intentions that are for the highest good of all.** When I started my life as a sadhaka, I accepted the idea that I would be a celibate, at least for the time, since I was not married. It was a terrific struggle for me as a young man, much of the trou-ble was brought on because I did not have the means to control my own mind.

There was another part that worked against me. I wanted to be in a relationship with someone. Of course, this is natural for most people, but since there was no one in my life in those years, I surrendered the idea to God as to whether it was to be my lot to find someone that was right for me, or not. I say I surrendered the idea, but what I should say, is that I worked to surrender the idea. I really wanted to have that special someone, but where was she!? This mixed nature in me, part surrendered, part holding on, made for mixed results. I was my own worst enemy in that I did not create in myself a pure intention. Really, I had mixed intentions. It is not that I did not try; I worked with all that I had to do it right. **As long as you have mixed intentions, you will get mixed results.** Much of spiritual sadhana is creating the pure intention that what you want is God-realization above all else. Sadhana is the purification of the mind toward this single intention.

To control the mind is to control the imaging, or imagining factor, in the mind. The mind constantly creates pictures: of the past, the future, what you want, what you desire, thoughts from the subconscious mind, all of it passes on the screen of your imagining mind. When intruding desire-thoughts come, and they will, what to do? Having created the intention of purity of mind, you will strike out every thought image not in concert with your goal.

X it Out

Whenever an image comes onto the screen of your mind that is contrary to your goal of brahmacharya, put a big black **X** in front of the image. Immediately replace that prior image with an image that is in concert with your goal. For instance, you may have an image of someone to whom you feel sexually attracted, immediately, put an X over that image. Then you bring to mind the image of yourself as the fully illumined one you created before. Then step into that picture and feel what it is like to be that illumined one, the freedom and bliss of that expansive Self. Or, you may see yourself sitting in a circle with the Masters all around you, feeling their influence and spiritual vibration. Never leave a blank screen after erasing the old image, for that invites the old desires to express new images on the screen of your mind. Be sure to feel what that new Self is like, for feeling creates the desire nature, and you want to desire God alone.

Avoiding

Everything felt in the body is a reaction to a stimulus and your interpretation of that input. Stimuli may be external, something you directly see, hear, feel, taste, or smell, or it may be an internal stimulus, a memory, projected idea, or dream. If you are dealing with external stimuli, you see someone attractive, smell something that creates desire, hear a stimulating voice, etc., you can avoid the stimulation or create a new association for it.

Sometimes avoiding is thought to be a bad word, but it can be very helpful when used correctly. Avoiding someone who stimulates desire is a good strategy. You know when you are playing with fire. When you have sexual energy for someone and you go out of your way to play with that energy, it goes against mental purity. When you find someone visually stimulating, you can look to the side or down to avoid visual contact. If you have good concentration, you can also be looking at the person with these two eyes but your greater focus is upon the ajna, the third eye. Also, you can avoid situations that bring you into close contact with someone you find attractive. Avoidance can be a very good tool to keep your mind on the right track.

Creating New Associations

In India, the men in the ashrams call all women "mothers." The new association is, "This woman is my mother" (a rather cooling thought to sex drive, warming to the heart). Or, "This woman is the Divine Mother," a sacred thought. And for women, "This man is my father, my baba, or papa." When you see all those of the sex you might have an attraction to as mother, or father, it changes the association.

When I worked in an antique store as a retail manager, I practiced mentally bowing down at the feet of all women who came into the store, seeing them as the Divine Mother. It became an automatic thing to do and helped me create new associations for all women.

Another way of using associations is to visualize a picture that produces a cooling effect. For instance, you might imagine someone without any skin! See that person as organs, bones, muscles, and blood vessels, all without any skin covering at all. Or, you can imagine him or her getting older and older, until very old, shrunken, wrinkled; and then to see the person die and turn into worm-infested bones as the body gradually turns to dust! This is all-out war!

Transmuting Physical Sensations

What creates desire nature is the feeling of pleasure that comes with an experience. When you feel the Bliss of God and recognize its superior nature over sensory experience, you have a desire more and more for God alone. For most sadhakas, desire is mixed. Part of you aspires for the higher nature of Bliss. Part of you is pulled to fulfill the desire nature of the senses. Through spiritual practice, you feel the Bliss of God more and more, and this becomes the predominant motivation for you. But bodily desires do not die overnight! The struggle over the psyche of the mind is terrific. All the great masters assure—persevere and you will reach your goal.

When physical sensations stemming from the sexual plexus get stimulated, either from exterior senses or interior images, the drawing power toward fulfilling sexual desire becomes very strong. Combining the power of imaging with the power of feeling, you can transmute this energy and then feel the wonderful results. Repeated practice of this begins to convince the mind of the wonderful qualities of Spiritual Nature.

Imagine, at the base of the spine, a series of nerves that lead to the sexual organs. In your mind's eye, trace those nerves back to the base of the spine. Imagine in the spine a switch that turns on or off the flow of life-force to the sexual nerves. Repression is when the switch is left on, stimulating the nerves with sensations, but the desire is not acted upon. Transmutation occurs when the switch is turned off and the energy is released to flow upwards into the spine and higher centers.

For example, you become aware that there are feelings of arousal in the sexual plexus. Mentally bring the focus of your attention to those nerves and trace them back to the spine. When sensitive, you can feel and "see" exactly where those nerves go and feel the energy being fed by the spinal powerhouse. When you locate the connection between the powerhouse in the spine and those nerves leading to the sexual plexus, you can imagine flipping a switch from the on-position to the off-position, or you can imagine a "Road Closed" sign (you can use any imaginative signal to the brain that your creative mind can come up with to indicate that the outward flow of energy is blocked). Now, just above that point in the spine, see a trapdoor that is closed, blocking the passageway further up the spine. Then, see that trapdoor suddenly spring open allowing the flow of energy streaming up the spine.

Now the subtle astral spine, the sushumna, is continuous from the base of the spine to the medulla oblongata. Realized yogis and spiritual masters know this through their own experience. You are taught to focus your attention on the heart center, the ajna, or the crown chakra. Bring that flowing energy to any one of these three points. See and feel that energy come upwards and express itself as love through the heart, merge into the Light at the ajna, or bring you into absolute union at the crown chakra.

In this way, you feel the superior joy of the soul expressing itself in these higher planes of consciousness. This positive joy and fulfillment create an association in the mind the soul would like to establish as a regular feature. Through positive attraction then, rather than by negatives alone, the transmuted sexual energy finds a new source of fulfillment. Complete union with God has been described as ten thousand orgasms happening at once! This powerful positive feature of transmutation opens new vistas, new frontiers.

And from the heart center and the ajna, creativity can flow in whatever way the Divine wishes to flow in you. Whether through words, art, voice, craft, healing, or silently loving the world, Divine life flows spontaneously through you to all. Without fetter or restriction, it uses your talents and abilities and raises them to their highest form. And the fulfillment comes not just with the outer expression of some art or science, but an inward joy is experienced through the action itself. Every moment lived in this way is a fulfillment to itself.

And when your life is filled with such moments, a spontaneous flow of Divine life, then you fulfill the real reason for which you were born. You no longer earn your living by the sweat of your brow—although your brow may sweat, you imbibe God's goodness, and by expressing it to all, He looks after your every need. You find yourself walking in the Garden of Eden, at one with your God, at peace with yourself, and in the knowledge of the oneness of spirit in all things, created and uncreated.

This, then, is the fulfilled life of a brahmacharya. No loss, do you feel. No separation or barriers, but oneness of Soul and Spirit are yours. This can be yours through the practice of brahmacharya.

The Body

There are means of doing exercises with the body that can also help in this transmutation. The Clearing Breath can be focused on the sexual plexus and base of the spine with good results.[12] Also, the Mahamudra in Kriya Yoga is designed to help transmute this energy. The Shoulder Stand and Candle Stand and exercises of Hatha yoga are good for reversing the usual downward flow of sexual energy. If one has the flexibility, one can sit in the Hero Pose,[13] then shift the weight to one side,

---

12   For full description see *Silence: Entering the Cosmic Sea of Consciousness,* The Cross and The Lotus Publishing (Appendix, pp. 502–535).

13   Another version is to sit in Hero Pose, bring one knee against your chest, then shift your weight and bring the heel in place.

placing the anal passage on top of the heel. Feel the energy moving up the spine.

Diet can also be important. In yogic thought, a spicy diet is not good for brahmacharyas—perhaps that is why the spicy Indians have a large population! Onions, peppers, and other spicy foods are to be avoided. You may notice other cause-and-effect foods: for example, too many creamy foods increase desire nature. Experiment with yourself, noting any cause- and-effect links between the foods you eat and your body consciousness.

I think it does not need to be said, but I will say it anyway: provocative pictures, performances, movies, and fantasies all go against mental purity. Even if it doesn't have any noticeable immediate effect, it goes into the subconscious mind and comes back later. If unavoidably caught in such circumstances, you can just look away and chant. Besides, by having God on your mind, you will probably have a better time of it than the attentive audience!

High Frequency Energy

All these practices and the transmutation of this energy can cause a high frequency of energy to flow up the spine. If it is not channeled properly, it can cause disturbances and imbalances. As mentioned earlier, the heart, ajna, and crown chakras are the best to focus on. Be responsible with this energy. If it is used for the wrong purposes, you will pay for it with karmic consequences. The safest way is to stay focused on God. Make that your goal and mantra. Create goodness and upliftment for yourself and others. If this transmuted energy is used to strengthen a rebellious will, if used to create ugliness and mischief, if used to promote ego-driven spiritual powers, then woe unto you. You will be the creator of your own self-made hell, as you will have to face the effects of everyone your thoughts and actions have reached. Let this only be for good and for God. If nervousness or increased mood swings occur, then seek to purify yourself by chanting God's name and finding positive creative outlets. If problems such as these are occurring, of course, you may contact anyone with an appropriate background to help in these cases. These words are not said to frighten, just guidelines for the "what ifs." I pray that God's blessings be upon you, that He lift you up and bring you to the realization of who and what you truly are through deepened prayer and meditation upon God alone. May it be so!

Spiritual Powers

From the beginning of time, humankind has sought to gain advantage for the promotion of its survival, comfort, some plan or ideal, or the domination of others. Through physical power, mental power, or spiritual power, this has been the way. Generally, one thinks of spiritual qualities such as universal love and service, experiencing joy, bliss, and surrender to the Higher Will as the qualities of a saint. But few of us can read the stories of great saints or spiritual masters and the apparent miracles that occur in their lives and remain unaffected. To be honest, it has to be said that this is an appealing feature in any anecdote of a spiritual master.

There may be one thing said in regard to spiritual powers. The difference between fully realized masters and those of some realization who use powers from an ego standpoint, is the fully realized master is indifferent to having such powers and only uses them by Divine command. No taint of pride, personal agenda, or attachment goes with any display of a mystical power.

It is proclaimed by all the great scriptures and masters that powers are to be eschewed. The temptation to delve into the world of powers is very seductive. High-minded souls can be drawn into thinking they can be of help to others through the use of extraordinary powers. The reality of such thinking soon shows itself; the powers are not serving us, but we are serving those powers. Emperor ego delights in having more than the fellow next door. And who are we to know what serving a good is? If we heal someone who is working out past karma through that affliction, do we not risk only postponing the inevitable, creating future difficulty for that person, perhaps with interest?

Only through God-given intuition may we know for certain that a certain act is the right thing to do. That is why Swami Ramdas said: "You can do no good until you are God-realized." This is an astounding statement, but true, at least in terms of us doing a predictable good. Because no one has sufficient information to be able to determine what will lead to a good. Does this mean we cease to act? No, of course not. But in our prayers, we should ask God to lead our reason, will, and activities according to His will, and then do our best to attune ourselves to that will. We do this until that time comes when we have dissolved the little self of the ego into the vast universal Self of God, and then even the ideas of "I" and "Thou" are no longer present, and going against God's will is not even a possibility.

If we take the attitude of the child when it comes to spiritual powers, then we are all right. "O Father, Mother, God, you do all through me. I know nothing of these powers; if it happens, it will happen automatically through me without my doing." Thus, will think the Bhakti, the devotionally minded aspirant. The Jnana yogi, guided by discerning intellect, will think, "O Infinite Spiritual Consciousness, all activities in this world are an illusion. Why would I trade one illusion of being helpless for another illusion of being powerful? I abjure them all!"

The Karma yogi will think, "O God, I serve all as your form. In fact, it is You, You, in this form who serves all as You, who exist in other forms. Therefore, I know of myself, I do nothing. It is You who doeth the works." And the Raja yogi proclaims, "O Infinite Self, powers come naturally to the yogi. It is an anathema to real spiritual progress. You may use this body as an instrument of Your will. I am neither attracted nor repulsed by the powers. What are they in comparison to You, the magnificent Existence both in this world and beyond?"

In this way, all four personality types of real sadhakas will strictly avoid egotistic use of powers. It may be said, there are two broad paths when it comes to the mystical. One is spiritualism: that is, contacting dead spirits and the development of occult powers. The other is spirituality, which is the cultivation of a surrendered ego for the purpose of realizing the ultimate Being, God. The two paths are polar opposites in where they lead the sadhaka. Many get involved in a spiritual path due to enticing stories about the development of occult powers. Through this interest, they come to a path whose focus is on Self-realization. So, they may have a mixture of attraction for spiritualism and a draw to spirituality. The beginner may fail to distinguish between the two! Of course, needless to say, the ego would like both! But since they lead to opposite goals, this is not possible. Cultivation of powers leads to the aggrandizement of ego. Spirituality, on the other hand, leads to the end of ego-consciousness and involution toward Divine Consciousness.

A decision must be made by the sadhaka. The more we rise in spirituality, the bigger and more tempting become the powers. There are very highly realized yogis who become derailed by the seduction of powers. So do not be deceived by progress on the path or a feeling of oneness with the Infinite, thereby above temptation. Become neutral to powers, neither attracted nor repulsed, for repulsion may be hiding a latent desire for powers. Rather, let's see ourselves as the indifferent instrument, and if it is His will, He will effect the change through us, with or without our knowledge. With this kind of surrender, we will be blessed with perfect peace and secure knowledge that it is indeed our Heavenly Father who doeth the works.

Dragons at the Door

A sadhaka has God-experience for some time, then gradually, or suddenly, falls from that high experience of peace or bliss and is immersed in worldly affairs. Like someone who has taken ill and cannot remember what it is to feel well, so the devotee becomes enmeshed in the world and either completely forgets God, or feels as though it were a dream. How does this occur, and why?

We have all come from God, the bliss, peace, and all-pervading Consciousness that is our natural state. The reason we become dissatisfied with the world is due to this deep subconscious memory of our oneness with God. I have talked to so very many people who have come from families that were like descriptions of hell. Yet, they held onto an idea that it should be different, and that idea (ideal) is so strongly embedded in them that they come to a spiritual teacher or a therapist with the idea of having something they know must be theirs, yet they have not had that experience. This ideal is common to so many, and yet most people do not even question why those with such a difficult background should think their life should be any different.

If we are a product of our environment only, then one would think we would be more accepting of the reality we have grown up with and not question it. Even if we were exposed to other families that seemed to be closer to that ideal, we might wish we had that, but we would not necessarily think, "That should be me." The reason for this ideal, this drive for something better, is because that ideal is fundamental to our makeup. At our core, the essence of who we are is resonant with that ideal, and we want our outer life to reflect that essence. It is the aberrant person, rather than the norm, who would not have a vision of something greater for themselves and their family: a life filled with light, peace, and wisdom. Even if we are not actively involved in creating this kind of life, and in fact living a miserable life and making others miserable to boot, yet this desire for light, peace, and harmony is pervasive.

But there are those who have a faith, an undying faith, despite all outer signals to the contrary (they may be called an idealist or an optimist), but they have not given up on this resonant thought, the essence of what we call Spiritual, or God. In faith, they start on a journey to find that ideal, to experience and live in Light and Harmony. Others whose faith has been shattered may jeer at those optimists, but the ones who have an undying drive go beyond what the world thinks of them. And because of that, they embark on a journey that takes them beyond the realm of the material. Their sincere desire brings them to a path that focuses their attention within. By going within they face their entire past. Those dark forces of the past are the dragons that stand guard at the door to the Eternal. Anyone who does not have the courage to face those dragons will not gain entry; every fear, every outward desire nature must be faced and overcome. This is not a journey for the weak of heart. One must have faith and courage, and a willingness to go on in the face of stiff opposition. Faith is perhaps the greatest weapon such pilgrims/warriors have at their disposal. This allows them to face these dragons (breathing their fire, casting their spells), using their faith as a shield and discrimination as a sword.

Layer after layer, they descend into the mountain deep. If sadhakas persevere, at last, they come to the lair of the dragon with the gold and gems of spiritual realization for which they have been seeking. But with each new discovery, enjoyed for a while, comes a new opponent.

Of course, in all of the opponents we are facing, it is really our very own self. On this journey of self-discovery, we must work to seek out those treasures of Spirit. Those treasures are ours already, but because we have, in memory dimmed past, placed obstructions along the way, we must face and overcome each obstacle. Through our past actions, we have set mind traps of negativity, greed, lust, jealousy, and hosts of other limiting and false beliefs. A narrow human view made us think at the time of their creation that there was no consequence to our actions or possibly no alternative to the way we lived our life. But once done, these thoughts, words, and actions of the past do not just disappear into the ether. They carry a life-energy with them, and they reside inside of us. They become a part of the sum total of our consciousness. Not until we rid ourselves of the idea of "I am the body" will these inner dragons be slain. When we realize, "I am Spirit, I am He," then all dragons will become nothing more than paper dragons. With a puff, these paper dragons may be whooshed away, carrying no more power than a fleeting thought.

Having discovered the spiritual treasure within, we make our ascent up the center of the mountain; there we will be lifted into the high realms of the Universal Vision. During this upward ascent, we are suddenly, at the speed of thought, dashed down to the ground; this is nothing more than the uncovering of other dragons jealous of their domain. Again, we make the ascent up, then something along the way captures our fancy, and like a helium balloon suddenly weighed down with a leaden basket, the upward ascent is stymied and brought back to the earth. These traps, sometimes subtle, sometimes frightening, sometimes tempting, run the whole gamut of human experience. Again and again, we seek to make that ascent. Again and again, we are brought up short. Only the intrepid, only the determined, only those who persevere beyond all obstacles may gain the goal.

Once we recognize that this up and down journey is part of the game and not peculiar to just us, we take away one of the most powerful dragon weapons: low self-esteem. This low self-esteem causes us to think, "I am the worst devotee because I have these thoughts, these fears, these desires, and all I want to do is hide!" And so, we hide away, away from our spiritual practice, our spiritually kindred spirits; we hide away from the Light. Of course, we cannot really hide, but we do try. All we succeed in doing in this hiding is to create more dragons, dragons of shame, and dragons of bad habits. We have just loaded more weight to the load we were already carrying. No wonder the world seems so heavy on our shoulders at times when we are carrying the weight of all those dragons.

Letting go of feeling worthless and letting go of avoidance, we proceed with faith that we are God's very own. We hold in our hands the sword of discrimination that cuts away that which detracts us from our journey to God; **eyes ever fixed on our journey's end, we will make progress and we will arrive at that ideal that has ever lived in our heart.** We are God's very own and no darkness, no obstacle, no dragon on the path will ever change that! Let us affirm our unity, our wholeness, and our all and all to that Divine Nature, and no obstacle will bar our path. Know, without any doubt, that at this moment we are the purity and power of absolute Spirit. If we do this with complete faith and surety, we will rise to the top of that mountain. And in so rising, we will behold that the whole world is nothing but a manifestation of that singular Spirit. We have ever been, we are now, and we will ever be completely and totally one with the Divine Consciousness of God.

The Razor's Edge

An inner fire of renunciation must burn clean and strong for the fullest God-Experience to be born within us. This fire of renunciation, coupled with a complete focus on God, will effectively purify the mind of attachment and make us attuned to God alone. The realization of God, however, is not usually gained in one jump, but is a process of purification. Even those who rise high in spiritual consciousness contend with dual forces, one going to God and one toward desire nature. Sadhana, the pathway to God, is walked, as the saying goes, on a razor's edge.

India, more than any other country or region in the world, has made a science out of realizing God. With clear descriptions of the various levels of consciousness in the divine realms, they give a roadmap by which we may be able to judge our progress. Along with seeking higher consciousness, these sages are giving the constant admonition to continue in strength and purity to the very end. The very end is what is called Sahaja Samadhi, a rare state of attainment where all opposing forces are once and for all absorbed into a unified state of realization. From this lofty height, the soul is free from a fall as it has attained a unity with the all-powerful and ever-pure Consciousness of God. This high goal is held out as the true purpose for taking birth and should be the supreme goal for all humanity.

When the soul is ready to make that final journey to God, a Sat-Guru comes into his or her life. This ancient and highly cherished tradition of the guru-disciple relationship is practiced all over the world, varying only in what it is called. Jesus acknowledged his past-life discipleship to John the Baptist when he said it fulfilled all righteousness that he should receive baptism from John. (Matthew 3:15) Krishna took instruction from his Guru, Sandipani. The guru is an instrument of the Divine to awaken the inherent Divinity within the receptive sadhaka. Even in the case of great Avatars, already perfected ones, the honoring of the guru tradition is evident.

At the point of entering upon this steep ascent of following the Sat-Guru, we are asked to sacrifice everything at the feet of God. Inner renunciation is essential to climbing these spiritual heights. This renunciation of the outer stimulation that once so attracted the mind allows for an inner magnetic draw of bhakti, or love and desire for God-experience, to take the sadhaka over. With growing desire for higher spiritual states, we feel ourselves to be in contact with realms divine. The oppositional forces, far from retreating from this field of battle, come on with greater intensity—fighting for life.

The path of realization is a series of ups and downs. Perhaps after a beautiful meditation, we float out of the door with feet barely touching the ground and the air has never smelled so pure, the flowers never looked so beautiful. Suddenly, a car angrily honks its horn, music blasts its raucous vibration from a neighbor's house, the crowd thickens and people are pushing to make their way through; the din of activity is crushing to the sensitized nerves! From that pure state of joy comes feelings of hurt, anger, and thoughts of revenge. Oh, how fragile that state, how easily we are drawn back into the world and even into negative states of thought and feeling!

Through dedicated practice, we gradually experience the higher states of bliss and expansion of consciousness, making us feel a part of everything that is. A broad universal love and empathy make us feel we are not just one body, but the bodies of all. Even while moving in the body, we feel in deep communion with this high state of consciousness. We have achieved some mastery of ourselves and are living more and more in Divine communion. At this point, we may feel we have made it—transcended the realm of duality and are living in the supreme state. This experience may last for hours, days, or extended periods of time. Then some desire nature beckons; something lying in the subconscious mind gets triggered. Continuing in the glow of this higher consciousness, devotees may come to see themselves above the laws of cause and effect, thinking that what they desire is what God desires through them.

This is a dangerous time for sadhakas. It is the time Jesus was referring to when false Christs will rise up and proclaim their pre-eminence. The sadhaka-master thinks, "Here is a desire, is it not the desire of God?" It is a great test to the sadhaka; back and forth goes the mind in trying to judge the rightness of the situation. The mind tries to reason, but reason sees both sides of the coin; perhaps there is reason to think that following this desire will do good for another or others. The desire is strong, and one feels strong in God; should the sadhaka follow the path of desire? This is the razor's edge.

The scriptures of the world and the lives of all saints are filled with the stories of temptation, of rises and falls. Even in the stories of such luminaries as Jesus and Buddha, times of temptation are narrated. Jesus fasted in the wilderness for forty days, then came a time of temptation. In the case of Jesus, the temptations concerned the power of performing miracles and having world dominion. Two very seductive temptations for the upward-bound master. The final temptation came for Jesus at the garden of Gethsemane when the annihilation of the ego, body consciousness, was at hand. Would it be human will or Divine Will? Jesus surrendered to Divine Will and the world has been the recipient of vast blessings as a result.

The Buddha too went through his night of testing. Mara came in the guise of young women to test the Buddha. Mighty soldiers came to threaten his body with war and destruction. He passed these tests, reposing in his Self, his true nature. As a result, he achieved Buddhahood, even as Jesus achieved Christhood. We know of their victories. Did they also have times of falling short of the mark, not overcoming the temptations? We are accustomed to stories of spiritual masters always making the right decisions. Of course, in the Old Testament, we have examples of those who made the wrong decisions and paid a price as a result. There are parallels in all scriptures where good, even great men and women of God, made the wrong choices.

What is tremendous about Jesus and Buddha is that in their overcoming, they attained the pinnacle of realization. With that Divine transformation, they achieved a wonderful Status—they went over the top, no longer subject to falls or making the wrong decisions.

But what of those masters, great in their own right, but who have not yet achieved Buddhahood or Christhood? What shall be said of them, and being tempted, do not make the right choice? Desires that lead to a fall can be in any field of human endeavor; they can be in the realms of gaining influential power, sex, money, psychic powers, gaining name or fame, even in the name of doing good. Whatever is most seductive, most alluring to sadhakas, will come with great power and seek to turn them away from advancing further in realization.

When this desire nature comes to sadhakas, reason, feeling, and all faculties may fail to help. It must be understood this can happen to souls in very high states of development. Having gained a great deal of self-mastery, they have moved into high states of consciousness. Others may look upon them as world teachers, spiritual masters, and they would be right to say so. But they have not gone over the top; they have yet to go to the supreme heights of Sahaja Samadhi, and they are yet in danger of a fall.

The fact that one who is recognized as a great master is subject to a fall can be disillusioning to sadhakas who have looked up to that one. They may feel betrayed, hurt, angry, lost, and forlorn. We have examples of some of the most famous spiritual teachers of our time, both East and West, subjects of scandal: sex, money, and power (both worldly and psychic) being the chief objects of temptation. Sadly, this has been one of the signs of our times. One cannot observe this without compassion for the innocent, those with faith in such teachers feeling crushed by such revelations.

And what of the master, what shall we say of him or her? Newspapers and gossips love some juicy news. They are willing to destroy anyone at the price of something to report, sometimes forgetting to note whether it is actually true or not! A reputation is thus destroyed, but rarely restored. The voracious appetite for scandal is really quite amazing. Others can then say, "See, none stand higher than any other," and in this way, they can support their own complacency. So, balance and fairness are not to be expected from such sources. We must have the means to make an evaluation, for we all make judgments of others, and when it comes to following someone's teachings, we should evaluate the one we follow.

Following the razor's edge is no small task. At times following that edge leads to a fall. Not every fall can be said to be equal. The complexities of the human mind and karmic patterns are wonderfully varied. Temptations and falls will represent a pattern of the subconscious mind. Temptation can be a lifelong preoccupation, or it can be some sudden eruption from the depths of consciousness. It is this polarized struggle through which each soul must pass. We have some brilliant examples of spiritual masters who shot to the top, but even they talk of spending years in becoming stabilized and balanced in that highest state. This is the great battle that all must wage, the crucifixion through which all must pass.

The outcome of such struggles, and falls, is not dictated so much by the power of the temptation, but by how the master deals with such temptations. A master may face a temptation and through the power of grace and self-mastery, not act on it, rising above it. This scene may be enacted again and again, but the master remains victorious. These virtuous ones are deserving of our highest praise. Others, attaining a level of mastery, may give in to temptation and become ensnared in its tangle for a little time, or a long time. The struggle is terrific. If the master emerges from the other side, he or she will have conquered the opposing force, and will become more stable in the refined God-Consciousness. These souls too, although temporarily tainted by their actions, end up victorious, gaining their complete emancipation.

Others do not come out of the struggle, but stay in it, not rising above, but not totally giving in to it either. Back and forth it goes with no absolute resolution. If they die with this struggle, they attain to the good reward they have earned, then return to another body to continue the struggle to gain total self-mastery. The other class of souls who struggle with darkness are those masters that do not rise above the struggle and turn from the light and lead the life of a lie instead. They no longer struggle, other than experiencing an occasional guilty conscience. The desire nature becomes institutionalized into their life. These individuals have given up any right to be called a master and are leading lives of darkness, not light.

It may come as a surprise to some that I would give the name master to one who has not attained total mastery. But the truth is, one can be in the realm of mastery and yet have more to pass through. Teachers may be a guru, a master, when they have become stable in the fifth chakra. This allows them the discernment for helping others to attain that exalted state. In fact, most of the world's teachers had yet to attain total mastery at the time they started their ministry to the world. "When such masters are in positions of authority, positions of teaching, should they not be perfect?" For many such masters, it is the fulfillment of their karma that they need to help others to their realization in order to become fully realized themselves. Hand in hand, the master and sadhaka walk the path to the Infinite.

There is a danger in the sadhaka misconstruing the truth of this teaching, thinking, "Falls happen, if I give into a temptation, it is no big deal." This would be a total misreading of the facts. One who turns away from the light pays the price; the law of karma is exact and immutable. Oftentimes masters, in their teachings, hold out only the highest, only the most perfect of realizations and do not mention recovery from falls when they are at high states of consciousness. The reasoning is, "Whatever is placed into the mind is what is then created. If only the most perfect attainment is taught, then the sadhaka will strive for and attain to that most perfect union." This is a great and noble teaching. However, there is a danger that the sadhaka, not being taught the nature of falls, will gain a false conception of the path. If sadhakas struggle with desire nature, even after attaining higher states of mastery, perhaps even having a fall, they may feel they are unworthy of spiritual realization; hence, the high teaching could actually retard the progress of sadhakas.

Sadhakas must hold the highest ideal and be realistic about the nature of the path at the same time. Like climbing a mountain, they constantly keep their mind on the peak, but remain also mindful of the ups and downs of the path through the foothills and the rocks on the path during the final steep ascent. Too much thought of the peak without paying attention to the path will lead to stumbles; too much attention to immediate surroundings and forgetting the goal of the peak will make sadhakas lose their way. **God is both the goal and the means to the goal.** So constant fixity of the mind on God, overcoming temptation, and seeing God as the absolute goal will keep sadhakas on the path in the best way.

We have the example of one guru who came here to the West and gained quite a following. He made it his specialty to collect very expensive cars. One of his ideals he put forward, in contrast to all the great teachings, was that if you have a desire, you should go out and fulfill it. I suppose one of his desires was for Rolls Royces and he was busy trying to get his fill of as many as he could. This abuse of his position, of course, was just the tip of the iceberg. He ended up going to further extremes to the point where his group was accused of attempting to poison the water supply of a nearby town, guards were carrying automatic weapons, and many other examples of adharma—unrighteousness. Some example of a spiritual consciousness!

It also must be clear that there are many misconceptions about mastery and the nature of being established in the fifth, sixth, or seventh chakras. Some teachers substitute being well versed in philosophy for being realized; others have some movement of kundalini, or some sensation in a chakra and say, "I have awakened that chakra," assuming they are then qualified to teach. Still others have some revelations, experiences in higher consciousness, or they gain some powers and think they are now established in the highest Consciousness. These are the many "false peaks" on the way to the pinnacle of realization. The true way of knowing we are growing in realization is the continuous state of joy and purity of consciousness we enjoy. Confirmation from a living guru, saints, and realized souls has the greatest value in these higher stages. The sure path to God is to keep our attention ever fixed upon Him and be in humble submission to His will. Only when communion with God is ongoing and perfectly established may we say we have attained the goal.

Another example of a fall from grace was some years ago when a young man from India came to America with an ability to reveal an inner light in the third eye to initiates. He attracted large crowds and grew in name and fame. Some scandal about him came into the news and his family started to quarrel about money and control; the whole thing fell apart. The seductiveness of power, name, and fame is quite intoxicating. Only through total renunciation and inner surrender to God and Guru may one safely pass through the maze of traps that lie in wait. Even with the best of intentions, teachers can fall miserably, hurting both themselves as well as many others.

So many aspirants have a sincere desire for spiritual awakening. There are many such instances where sincere devotees were willing to put their trust and faith in one, only to be let down. It is a crime perpetrated against their souls and is of the most serious nature for both teacher and student. Many teachers are quick to claim they are beyond the law of cause and effect and thus excuse their behavior. The fact is that in most cases, even when a genuine master has risen above the law of karma, they continue to practice right behavior as an example to those coming up the ladder. They know how easy it is to slip off the narrow way and they want to be the example of one who leads an exemplary life.

Until the time we are fully established in that highest state of Sahaja Samadhi, we are subject to falls. We may be best guided by the wisdom of saints and scriptures: the basic dos and don'ts. If we should have a fall, then our immediate response is to pick ourselves up, brush off the dirt and blood, make reparations where possible, and get going back on our path to God. If we fall again, we get up again; we never give up, we never give in!

We must strive with all our strength, heart, mind, and soul to "be perfect, even as our Father in heaven is perfect." (Matthew 5:48) If we have some question about an inner prompting, as to whether it is from God or from lower desire nature, then we should submit it to our living Guru or a living God-man or God-woman. If these are not available, then we guide our lives by the scriptures, or by going within and seeking out the truth. If we are sincere and miss the mark, our sincerity will guide us back to God and the truth will be revealed to us.

Spiritual masters are here to lead us and help us get to the goal. If they are sincere and fall on the way up, then we should give them our compassion and our prayers for strength and clarity, letting it be a reminder of the need for absolute purity on the path. From the *Autobiography of a Yogi*, we read about the touching humility of the Guru toward the chela when Sri Yukteswar asks Yogananda, "If you ever find me falling from a state of God-realization, please promise to put my head on your lap and help bring me back to the

Cosmic Beloved we both worship."[14] When is a soul more in need of the strength and compassion of another soul than when they have fallen? Even highly realized masters can make errors; that is the time that all need to come together in strength, love, and prayer.

If we come to see that the master is not who or what he or she should be and has crossed over the line of deserving our respect or discipleship, then we take it again as a living example of what not to do and continue to strive for that inner perfection of God. Lest we be too quick to judge masters, let us look at the fruit of their lives. Do they lead others to God, or to themselves? Do they take full accountability for their actions and make sincere efforts to recover from a fall, or are they only stumbling from one fall to another? Are they humble, submissive to God and Guru, or are they arrogant and full of superiority? If the answer is consistently in the right direction, toward God, then they are leading us to the goal, even if with some faltering. If they are not, then better to shake their dust off our feet and continue on our way.

This life of the razor's edge is the most demanding we will encounter. Let us ever keep the highest goal in mind, while recognizing that human nature will be at play as the opposing force. Let us ever keep our purity of purpose, the fire of true renunciation, and real aspiration for God ever as our guide. The more perfectly we keep our mind on God, the surer and more direct will be our way to the goal. Let us ever strive with all our heart, mind, and strength, and ever pray for that all-powerful grace to lift us and keep us in that most perfect union with God.

Victory to God, Victory to Gurus, Victory to sadhakas everywhere!

---

14   *Autobiography of a Yogi* (pp. 94–95).

A Songbird's Verse

My life is a dedication to God. In fumbling steps and in the precision of movement, I steer my life toward that precious Goal. My great Guru set the course, direction, and Goal; she beckons me still from Her deeper life.

God awakened me to that purpose when my own will would have taken me to self-destruction, or at best to a mundane, senseless life. I pretend no greatness, nor even goodness, for there is none other good than my Heavenly Father. Truly, I can say whole-heartedly that it is by God and Guru's grace that I have found my Self.

I suppose it is natural to want all the world to share in that sacred mystery that I feel, and it would be sheer arrogance to assume no others do. But there is the songbird within that bursts into Divine verse and aches to share that deepest Intimacy, yet finds that longing all the more painful as its song disappears into the void. The pain is nothing but God's constant yearning for His children to forsake their gloom-drenched dream of creation long enough to join once again in Divine Union.

Songs of angels are not just beautiful voices, but the thrill of vibration that resounds throughout all space and is caught, and finds resonance in, the receptive soul. Like strings and reeds of various instruments, the soul feels the thrill of that glorious vibration. Thrill after thrill moves the soul, then settles into a quiet pool of peace.

A whispered breeze of joy gently plays on the surface of that quiet water; then a giant whale of inspiration rises above the surface, coming from great depths, revealing a portion of its massive body; then it sinks down below the surface once again. All nature, all existence is seen to thrill in ecstasy as a single life in various motions.

The heart heaves under the burden of the fruit it bears; the little mind is stilled, and the great Mind encompasses all as its own. No boundaries are there, circumference melts into Infinitude; peaceful, gentle, powerful, intimate, and expansive states of Being exist simultaneously in total harmony.

The Divine Song moves in the ether in constant waves, but ears and eyes are dulled to its tune by muddy coverings of earthly preoccupations, those reeds and strings of the soul dampened by material desire. O children of the Infinite, awaken to your vast mansion within! Let your souls sing in mystic vibration the thrilling tones of your Soul's Song. To die to the vain preoccupation of separateness is to resurrect into your vast, dimensionless Self:

No birth, no death, nor body am I,

I AM HE! I AM HE!

Blessed Spirit, I AM HE!

I AM HE! I AM HE!

Blessed Spirit I AM HE![15]

Let this be our anthem, our affirmation, and our realization. Die in our surrender to the Infinite Creator, our Heavenly Father, and resurrect in our perfect oneness with God alone.

What is in a Word?

What is in a word? Swami Sri Yukteswar wrote in *The Holy Science*, "The Almighty Force *Shakti*, or in other words, the Eternal Joy *Ananda*, which produces the world, and the Omniscient Feeling, *Chit,* which makes this world conscious, demonstrates the Nature *Prakriti* of God the Father."[16] In some later editions published in America, an enterprising editor decided that Sri Yukteswar did not know exactly what he meant in his own writing and interpolated the word "produced" for "produces." The

---

15   Adaptation of verse by Adi Shankaracharya.

16   *The Holy Science*. (1949). Jnanavatar Swami Sri Yukteswar Giri, Chapter 1, Sutra 2. Yogoda Sat-Sang Society of India, 3rd Edition.

variance of words represents two very different perspectives and demonstrates the beauty and sanctity of a Perfect Master's words.

In saying that God produces the world, Sri Yukteswar reveals a dynamic creation, not a static conception. In a dynamic sense, the world is constantly being created. Moment to moment, the Creator projects forth the idea of creation, keeping it aloft with His preservative power. One may ask, "Where does this creation come from?" The answer coming from realized saints is that creation is a manifestation of the absolute, unmanifest Spirit, sometimes referred to as the Void.

In order to grasp more clearly the relationship between the unmanifest Spirit and creation, we need only look to our own creative process. When we sit down to create, whether it be a writing, a drawing, whatever the creation, where does that creative idea come from? We can say, "It just came to me," or "I got the idea from seeing what someone else did." But when we are truly creative, original, where did that originality come from? Again, we may say, "The idea just came to me," but where was that idea before that? Did it exist before it "just came" to you?

Yogic science tells us it did exist before; something does not come from nothing. This unmanifest Void is not an empty nothingness. Rather, it is all that is in potentiality. What is manifest today as this earth, the trees, animals, and people, may be said to be just a fraction of all that is in potential. An author can illustrate a simple example of this. An accomplished author may have penned many volumes of books. When an author is writing something new or looking over something written before can we say all those volumes written are from him or her? Can we say they are in the author, and even more volumes exist yet to be written? But in that moment of time, all the author's attention is reduced to a single sentence or even a single word. In that moment of time, all that potential of what has been written and what is yet to be written is in the invisible void of the author.

In the same way, God produces His creation. Focused on a moment of time, on one particular aspect, He creates in this moment out of the infinite potential of what He is. And that creation is us, as we read these words. The thing that is amazing to the human mind is that God is simultaneously aware of creating the billions of people who inhabit this earth along with all the animals, vegetables, minerals, and every aspect of all creation, and He is equally aware of all that lies in His unmanifest potential as well. As God writes His play of creation, of which we are a part, He does not create something and then leave it behind, such as the author may leave written works behind in leather-covered volumes. There is no "leaving works behind" for God; there is only what is.

God is actively manifesting all that is at all times; if He was not, it would dissolve back into the unmanifest void the instant He did not actively sustain it. This act of preservation is the second principle of creation. In Yogic thought, there are three such principles. The first principle of manifested creation is the creative principle that brings all that is into being. The second is the preservative principle, and the third and last is the destruction principle that withdraws all creation back into the unmanifest void from which it came. These three principles are constantly at work in all creation, and they are constantly at work in us as well.

It is from our human perspective that we can look about ourselves and see stability in the world. Day after day we awaken to a world that appears very much the same. If we have lived in the same house for a long time, we can see the preservative principle at work. Those valuable treasures we piled in the garage are still there after years of trying to forget that we ever put them there in the first place. The preservation principle makes it appear to the human mind that God must have created this world, put things into place, and then left them there. This concept is pure delusion. The preservative principle freezes the creative projection as a trick of the mind in sequential moments of time. It is like looking at the creation and destruction of the world in a slow-motion movie scene. The projection of the creative principle is constant, or it would not be appearing to us. Destruction is the withdrawal of that projected creation back into the void, and it is also constant. Preservation is the appearance of that creative projection maintaining stability as a static state. It is a fact that God "produces the world" constantly and it is, therefore, a misperception that He "produced the world" in the past tense as a fait accompli.

What does that mean to us in a practical sense other than making a fine philosophical point? In order to see this creative principle in its true state, we must awaken ourselves from the preservative complacency of mind. Because of the preservative principle at work, things become familiar, and we come to believe a thing is known to us because it is familiar. This familiarity is necessary so that we are not in a constant state of disoriented confusion. This same familiarity tends to breed contempt. Because something is known, is familiar, we grow complacent with it; we take it for granted. We cease to see the marvel of its newness and we cease to be in awe of its destruction. A mind-numbing sameness can chloroform the mind into sleepwalking in this life: "Oh, it's just another day, going to work, driving home, just the same old thing." This lack of active awareness at the newness of life, its vitality constantly at work as seen in the miraculous nature of a flower, a newborn life, blinding us to the withdrawing power of dissolution, makes us the walking dead. We cease to see God's hand working in every aspect of creation.

This creation is not something, as some suppose, that God produced and then left in the hands of the devil. And it is not, as many materialists suppose, a creation that came from inert exploding gases, a happenstance expression of nature, devoid of meaning. This life, our life, is a marvelous expression of Divinity, full of meaning, ever new and alive beyond the comprehension of the human mind alone. To awaken to the fact that God produces the world moment to moment is to be alive to the idea that God creates us moment to moment. We are an active manifestation of God, an expression of God—God living His life through us! This is not the "same old thing" of life. To awaken to this dynamic nature of God is to awaken to that creative principle within our Self.

So many people become insensate to this aliveness. To realize that each moment is an active expression of Divinity puts us in touch with the vitality of our own Divinity. Worry, preoccupation with the world, fears, and desire nature, all have the habit of putting us to sleep in this active creative principle. There are times when we will awaken to the idea that we are missing this aliveness in our lives. It is at those times when we wish to leave everything we've created and start out new. The sad fact is that unless there is a deep change in our mental nature, we'll sustain the newness of life but for a short amount of time, then recreate the old sameness with clock-like regularity. Radical changes do not often match the hoped-for outcomes.

Aliveness, divinity, is a part of everything that is, and is embedded in our life right now. To awaken to it is to awaken to the fact that God is creating in us right now. To connect to the power and intelligence of that potential requires our simple acknowledgment of the fact that God is producing us now. By actively looking for that connection in life now and making the moments of our day count, we will know that God is living in our heart. We no longer count ourselves among the walking dead—we woke up, became alive to the great Divinity manifesting within us and all around. We do not sleepwalk through our life only to awaken at the death of the body and think, "Why did I not awaken during my life? Why did I sleepwalk through it as if it had no greater meaning?"

God is moving in us now as the intelligence with which we are reading these words. He is creating in us this very moment. We are He in human form. Arise, Awake! Know this fact beyond any mind-numbing, outward, worldly fact that has been accepted as reality. In awakening, we will know that Life, that Intelligence and that Joy, which produces all creation through all time. May that blessing be true for us now, with every turn of the page, in every sentence, and saturating every word of creation that produces our life.

Unlimited Power

Obstacles come into our life but for one reason: to make us draw on and grow into the Infinite power within us and make it manifest. Whether the problem be one of the body, relationships, work, or any situation we are in the midst of, we must realize we are not of limited, but of *unlimited*, potential. Strength doesn't come by having power over others or access to a large bank account; true power is the manifestation of that inherent Spirit within us.

Tests come to us as a challenge to our faith. Those who lack faith repeat to themselves, "I have not the means," and so they don't. Times come in everyone's life when opposition rises up and enshrouds the soul as a dark cloud. At that time of darkness, the test of the soul reaches its greatest climax—a profound test of faith.

There have been many great souls who have faced that cloud of darkness and with faith in their own power to overcome, have gone on to do great things. There is even a higher class of souls who, when faced with that dark night, have submitted themselves to their Divine Source and manifested a higher order of Spiritual power. In our survey of history, it is plain to see that the most powerful men and women in society have relied on that Divine Source.

The reason for this noticeable difference of results, between reliance on humans alone and reliance on God, is due to the perceived source of power. When individuals perceive the source of strength as in themselves, it is by its very nature limited, no matter how grandiose their vision. When individuals acknowledge their source of power as Divine, then they know no limit to the resources upon which to depend. Divine power, being unlimited, makes the individual an agent of unlimited power.

The other limiting factor for human expression of power is the limit of human intentional will. When a person seeks the accomplishment of some task, some goal, it has a certain circumference of thought, limited by the vision and imagination of the individual. However, when individual will is surrendered to Divine Will, then the unlimited nature of the Divine Mind may be brought to bear with its unbounded vision. The third and most crucial factor is human acknowledgment of the Divine Source; this power provides unerring direction for the use of power. Human nature is self-centered and tends to cater to what is good for the individual apart from the whole.

Divine Consciousness is ever aware of the whole and Its interest is in the good of the whole. Therefore, Its guidance to the surrendered mind brings about conditions that are for the highest good of all.

The combination of unlimited power, will, vision, and unerring direction produces the greatest potential in human experience. Whether it be the life of Krishna, Buddha, Jesus Christ, or any of the many saints and realized Beings who have moved this world, and have the power to move it still, we observe that they stand as living testaments to the superior power of the Divine.

These examples lie in contrast to the many great rulers who led in their own names. These men and women, some of whose names are known to us today, do not have the power to move us today in the same way as the previously referenced illumined ones. Many of the great and good men and women of the past we may admire, but greater by far are those who surrendered to their Infinite source.

A greater contrast can be drawn between those fully surrendered to the Divine and those powerful leaders who worked contrary to the Divine Light. One such leader who showed great promise, but betrayed his higher calling, was Napoleon. Napoleon brought many enlightened ideas and programs to his country. Many admired his ideas and viewed him as ushering in a new, more enlightened, era. Then, upon his coronation as emperor, he took the crown from the Pope's hands and placed it upon his own head.

This act was not just a dispute between a church official and a self-made ruler. The statement made by this act went beyond the wrangling for worldly power; it acknowledged man the ruler, disconnected from Divine submission. Even though Napoleon was at the height of worldly power at the time of his coronation, with that act he sowed the seeds of his own limited rule. All truly great leaders have known the Divine as the source of their power and lived in a humble submission to this fact.

A leader from this same era who displayed that humble submission is George Washington. He knew his reliance on Divine Providence was essential to success and enforced this among his troops. After the war, when offered the crown of absolute power, he repeatedly refused it. Rather, he accepted leadership reluctantly and set the pattern for peaceful succession when he gracefully surrendered authority of his own will. He stands as a unique example in modern times, in humble service to the greater good of a nation and to God.

In ancient India, there are stories of Rajas as absolute rulers, surrendering their throne, wealth, and power and leaving their kingdoms behind in order to practice spiritual discipline and gain enlightenment under the guidance of a guru. These Rajas were not only kingly in worldly attainment but became Rajas in Spirit as well.

Each of us is a leader whether we have a position of authority or purely by the "authority" of our own example. Every life is an experiment in realizing unlimited Spiritual power. This experimentation takes place in the human and Divine fields of experience. The discovery that we have unlimited power in the Divine comes as a revelation to a disbelieving human mind. For most, the mind slowly grows in faith and humble submission to Divine guidance and power.

Few humans have had to face such hopelessness, despair, and tragedy as George Washington had to endure in eight long years of war. But when we, in our own dark night, face those moments of difficulty, we may firmly rely on Divine Providence as our source of strength to go through that darkness and overcome all obstacles. Affirming unlimited spiritual power, will, and vision, we may rise to new heights, realizing that in God we have power and wisdom beyond measure. Even as clouds covering the earth have no effect on the sun, so do dark nights of the soul have no effect on the inherent Light and power we have in God. With full faith, we know this truth of our being and claim it as our own!

At all times, and especially in times of difficulty, let us go into deep communion with Infinite Source; accept no limitation to that Divine power and see our "bank account" of Spiritual power as full. Then, in surrender to Divine Will, turn ourselves over to its power, direction, and workings. Let us renounce all thoughts of negativity and align ourselves with Light. Every experience takes us closer to God and His unlimited bounty. We are the reflected child of that unlimited Source, the All and All in All.

The World is a Reflection of Your Consciousness

The world you see and interpret is very much a mirrored reflection of your consciousness. A walk through the woods and hearing someone's description of what they see will tell much about their consciousness. A hunter will describe the game found in the woods, good places to hunt, places for the blinds, etc. A photographer will look at angles, lighting, and the framing of shots. A military man will see good places to ambush, areas to array troops. An engineer will observe the mechanics of nature, and an architect, the design. Each will see the woods through their own peculiar filter of understanding.

Sadhakas can tell a lot about themselves or another person by what they consider worth observing about life in general, how it is observed, and what conclusions are made. For sadhakas, a unique view of the world begins to emerge with their practice. Many of the familiar filters of the mind will remain intact. The architect continues to notice design, the engineer, function. However, a peculiar link is formed in the mind regarding the source and reason for the form and function of a certain thing. All form, all function, all activity is seen as having one source and one ultimate purpose stemming from the supreme creative Intelligence of God.

If you are in the market to buy a car, you will narrow your choices to a few models, perhaps one make and model only. Due to your focus on that make and model of a car, you begin to pick out that car wherever you go. Your interest drives what you observe. By focusing on the Divine, you will see it manifest everywhere. The sadhaka-businessman is not only seeing a product produced, marketed, and revenues generated, but sees the movement of God as the creativity, intelligence, and power that makes it all possible.

When you let go of the idea that you are the doer and are but a mere instrument of that Divine Source, then you see with amazement and childlike innocence all that occurs in the world. Without guile you can operate in the world: "Wise as serpents, harmless as doves." (Matthew 10:16) Far from rendering you useless to the world, spiritual life makes the best of whatever occupation chosen. Sensitive to the movement of God-Consciousness, you open yourselves to creativity, focused attention, enthusiasm, integrity, and loyalty that makes for excellence in your field. By fulfilling the purpose for which you are born, you work in the world not just for personal gain but also as a means of bringing your light of God to all.

This makes for good business and professional development. No artificial barrier should be placed between work life and spiritual life. As Mother used to say, "When you are in business with God you are in business with all of life," because there is but one source for all of life and that is God. Therefore, God is interesting—you know that because the world is interesting. God is complex, He has many nuances. God is fun and dramatic. The essential things of God are simple and close to the heart. In short, God is all of life.

God cannot be removed from the world; He cannot be relegated to dusty books or be confined to a Sunday service. Unless your spiritual life permeates every breath taken, every thought, every action, you have yet to fulfill your sadhana. Someone may say, "Aren't you being a little extreme here? It's all right to be religious but let's not go overboard!" But that is the voice of someone who has yet to realize that God is not remote and aloof from human affairs. When you realize that God moves, is responsible for, and controls every aspect of life, then you know there is no part of your life God does not affect.

Not only is God part of all life, but He is also bliss, and all life is permeated with that bliss. Spontaneous joy, peace, and freedom are to be had for one attuned to this great life. Spiritual Consciousness does not subtract from life, but only adds a wondrous dimension of happiness for which all yearn. Many only deny themselves access to this dimension of bliss, Light, and freedom by clinging onto the old notions of separation from God. It is time to gain that union with God and awaken to who and what you really are.

There are pictures that have faces and objects hidden in the drawing. In the rocks and trees, your mind gradually identifies a face, an animal, all sorts of images you realize have been hiding in the picture. Once your mind identifies the picture in a picture, you can no longer avoid seeing the hidden picture. Your spiritual life is like that. Once you see the hand of the Divine moving in all creation, proceeding from one image-experience in life to another, every scene of your life gradually becomes imbued with that sacred Divine Presence of the All in All.

With this, enjoyment of life multiplies by many, many times. No longer do you find life boring, empty, or mundane. The mundane becomes Divinity manifest in all of its beauty, power, and intelligence. Boredom could no more be a part of your life than stagnant water be a part of a waterfall. All of life becomes a movement of joyous expression. Even loss, tragedy, and grief are viewed in a new way.

With perfect knowledge that all happens for a purpose and is working for your ultimate higher good, lose fear and gain peace. Difficulties and hardships draw you closer to the Light within through deepened prayer and communion with God. Comfort, guidance, and sustenance for the soul are found in that communion; in deep faith know you are part of a Divine Plan of goodness, whatever the appearances of life's situations.

A charming and instructive story about Mataji tells us much about her wonderful personality. She worked from early morning straight through to late night, serving Papa and all sadhakas who came to the ashram. At night, Mataji would ask Papa to read the newspaper to her. Of course, newspapers then, as now, are filled with the world's woes and tragedies. Her head would be nodding to sleep as Papa read. Finally, Papa said, "Mataji, every night you have me read you the news. You are tired, why don't you go to sleep?" "Because," Mataji explained, "when I hear about these tragedies it is my only opportunity to pray for those people." Isn't that a wonderful attitude? It really changes the way you listen to the news if you employ that. It changes *you* as you hear the news. As you enter into deep prayer for those afflicted, it not only changes you and helps those being prayed for, but it also puts out a vibration that helps to positively change this world.

There are more and more studies confirming the power of prayer. One hospital study observed a control group of patients for whom no prayers were being offered; another group of patients was the object of a prayer group. The doctors and nurses were unaware that a study was being done, and thus had no idea who was being prayed for. Those doing the praying did not personally know any of the patients. The study showed that those who received the prayers spent less time in the hospital, had fewer medications administered, and recovered faster than the control group. The scientific community is at last gathering evidence for, and taking seriously, the power of prayer.

Behavioral psychologists like to say you are a product of your conditioning by the world. It is true, of course, that your experiences in the world color your perception and understanding. Realized masters call these samskaras, or conditioning from the past, including past lifetimes. Through stilling the mind, these spiritual masters have penetrated deeper into the psyche than has the influence of worldly conditioning. These sages intuitively perceived that the physical brain is an instrument of a transcendent spiritual consciousness. The brain is not the creator of consciousness, but is actually the result of the primary builder, God-Consciousness. This is a reversal of understanding of cause and effect from the physical scientist's point of view.

Your intelligence, and life itself, is the result of the Divine Source of your being. The material mind seeks life "out there," out in the world of the senses, but the spiritual mind seeks life and abundance within, within the being—not outside. The conscious mind is inhibited from an inward search by a glut of sensory experiences. When the eyes are closed in concentration, distractions continue to disturb the brain as an "echo" of worldly vibration. Only in stillness is the mind illumined with spiritual Light. This is why the material mind is seen as darkness, and in opposition to God, the intuitive Divine Mind.

By focusing the mind within and upon God, the brain becomes illumined with the Light of this Divine Consciousness. As your mind is illumined with Light, you see your inner world and this outer world filled with Light. "The light of the body is the eye: if therefore thine eye be single, thy whole body shall be full of light. But if thine eye be evil, thy whole body shall be full of darkness." (Matthew 6:22) A quick test will reveal the nature of your consciousness. When you close your eyes and go within, do you perceive the light of your own being, or are you engulfed with darkness? Look out on this world: Do you see the light of spirit shining in all?

In the *Gospel According to Thomas*,[17] purported to be the original sayings of Jesus found in some caves near Nag Hamadi, Upper Egypt, we read a very interesting description of the kingdom of heaven:

> Jesus said: "If those who lead you say to you: 'See, the Kingdom is in heaven,' then the birds of the heaven will precede you. If they say to you: 'It is in the sea,' then the fish will precede you. But the Kingdom is within you, and it is without you. If you know yourselves, then you will be known and you will know that you are the sons of the Living Father."

> His disciples said to Him: "When will the Kingdom come?" Jesus said: "It will not come by expectation; they will not say; 'See, here,' or 'See there.' But the Kingdom of the Father is spread upon the earth and men do not see it."

I once went to my Guru with a problem that was disturbing me at the time. I said, "Mother, I feel God greatly inside of me as a Presence, as peace and bliss. But I do not see Him in the world. In fact, I find the world disturbing to me." Mother said, "First, you find God within you, then as you grow in God, you find Him everywhere." That helped me to see I was on the right track but had not completely reached my goal. (The second part I knew already; it was the confirmation I was on the right track that was so helpful!)

As the mind is purified, it becomes filled with Light on an ongoing basis. First, that Light is seen within, then it is seen in all creation. The Kingdom of the Father truly is spread upon the earth and not seen. But when you do see it, you enter into that realm and know that you are the son of the living Father. The Light that fills your Being is then known to be the same Light that you see in all

---

17   *The Gospel According to Thomas* (Saying 3 and 113).

creation. It is the good news, the gospel, that John the Baptist and Jesus brought for one and all: the kingdom is here; it is now, within you and all about you!

Saints and mystics have understood this power of the spiritual life for thousands of years. They have known that the Universal Vision of God produces the greatest happiness for you, or any individual. It also makes you ideal for your chosen work and benefits all the people in your life. It has the power to transform how you see this world. As your mind is illumined with Light, you see this world filled with that same Light. You come to really know that how you see this world is a reflection of your consciousness.

Plateaus

In any sadhaka's journey, there will be plateaus. A plateau, in a physical sense, is an elevated level piece of ground. In spiritual consciousness, a plateau occurs after gaining some elevation, some higher consciousness, and then a feeling of flattening out; a kind of status quo is established. Now in all growth, there are natural plateaus: a vigorous building period followed by a time of consolidation and rest. This is true throughout all of nature.

In the natural cycle of building and growth, there comes a point where either the cycle shifts from rest and consolidation to building once again, maintaining the earlier momentum, or else if one stays too long in one place, one tends toward becoming inert, sluggish, not able to move. If you are out on a hike, for instance, and you have been scaling a fairly steep climb, the body will benefit from a certain amount of rest, recharging blood cells with oxygen and carrying away waste; having brought the overall system into balance, once again you are prepared to continue the climb. But, continue the rest beyond a certain time and the energy required to get the body in motion again needs to be multiplied many times. The one who works in physical labor knows he cannot take too long a lunch break for this very reason.

Inertia is a two-edged sword. It maintains forward momentum when in motion, but it is also the tendency to remain still when at rest. A strong man used to demonstrate his strength by pulling so many train cars harnessed to him by a chain. With great strength and will power, he would strain to break the inertia of the stationary cars. Once the inertia of the train of cars at rest was overcome, he found the momentum of the moving cars made the next steps easier than the initial steps. The hardest part of the demonstration was overcoming the inertia of the cars at rest; it was relatively "easy" to keep them going after that.

These outer examples help you to examine the less visible inner world of Spiritual growth. Plateaus can be a time of needed recuperation, or they can become a place of eternal rest! The negative aspect of a plateau is that it can become like a train of cars at rest to which you are chained, needing incredible strength to get going again. The law of mind states: *with your thoughts, you are always creating.* Every idea that crosses the threshold of thought carries a spark of energy with it. It may be a little or a big spark; it may be a singular thought or there may be a legion of them. A negative habit can be like the proverbial poor relatives who come to visit; suddenly, all their children and dogs and cats have invaded the house, all with the stuck inertia of *not* moving out! You may assess your current trend by asking yourself: "Am I putting real effort into my sadhana? Taking a bit of a needed rest? Stuck on a plateau? Or am I plunging into descent?"

With a little honest reflection, you can make this assessment at any time as to the nature of your thoughts and the power or energy behind them. The power of habit will be your default mode, so whatever your past habits have been, that will be what you return to if you do not stay focused on the new pattern you are working to create. Since an evolving soul is working to get free of samskaras (habits from the past that keep you bound), then without active spiritual effort, your tendency will be to go to those old habit patterns.

In most cases, your past is dominated by body consciousness and your psyche is oriented around the ego. You must then have sufficient spiritual spark, a drive and enthusiasm for spiritual growth. If you do not, then not only will you hit a plateau and stay there, but there will be a tendency to head back downhill. Attitudes such as, "Well, I know I should meditate more, but you know, my life is so busy and when I get home, I just want to watch some television (for 2 or 3 more hours). After all, I work hard, don't I deserve some rest?" The excuse-making may take a myriad of appearances; but as I say, a quick assessment will let you know if you are taking a needed breather, if you have overstayed your break time, or if you are running headlong back down the hill!

And if you have lost forward momentum, what then? One of the aspects of lost momentum is the associated thoughts that come with it: "This is all really too much; I have worked so hard and gotten nowhere. This old life is really not so bad. You know, I am just so darn busy now. Maybe later in my life, then I will make more of an effort." One idea that comes when we are really looking for an out is, "Well, I think that spiritual stuff and meditation was a kind of phase in my life; I have moved on to other things now." In response to this, I would ask, "How can your search for the source of your Being, the source of all life, beauty, love, creativity, and of everything there is, be called a phase?" Surely, nothing so important can be thought of as a phase. The honest truth would be more becoming to a one-time earnest sadhaka.

These thoughts creep into the mind and are soul-destroying. That is, they undermine your spiritual search and aliveness. Living in this world, but not being of it, is a terrific challenge. There is no one keeping score; there is no one to please but yourself, but you should be honest with yourself as to what you are deciding in any moment. Decisions are important, and they determine your future.

You must be willing to face the consequences of your decisions, and by doing that consciously in this moment makes you more keenly aware of the importance of such decisions. One way to cut through all the noise of mental chatter, the pull of past tendencies, etc., is to project to the time when you will leave the body, the time of death. As you mentally project forward to that time and you look back over your life, make an assessment of your life. How did you live your life? What did you spend your time on? How satisfied are you with your decisions?

This perspective of the afterlife will be more closely attuned to your Soul's values. The pull of past habits can become intense and become even more so as you try to pull away from them. The reason that most aspirants fall short of the goal is not for any reason other than a spiritual indifference that creeps over the mind. This indifference is the plateau, and it has a great force to it. There must be a greater force exerted to overcome the past than the force the past has on you today. Where did that force of past habits come from? From yourself. Your own combined thoughts and actions have culminated in this great magnet of the past that pulls you back towards itself.

To remain oriented to where your soul's values are, you should associate with other spiritual souls. The magnetic field of one who is awakened, or is in the process of awakening, spiritually magnetizes your pull to things spiritual in a positive way; conversely, it weakens the pull of things worldly. Every soul goes through times of doubt, times of plateaus, times when the old life pulls with incredible force. The fact that these things act on you is not a sign of having fallen, or that the spiritual path is not right for you. This pull from the past is, in fact, a sign you are, like Arjuna, on the spiritual battlefield. You are caught between the opposing forces: one pulling toward God, one pulling you away.

Every day, deepen your prayer so that you will be graced with increasing desire for God alone. Even when enthusiasm burns madly for realization, pray for more. Why? Because every thought, every moment, is a creation; you are either increasing or decreasing. And while there may be the occasional rest, be like the first-string basketball player put on the bench: his whole attention is on the game and desire to get back into the game. Every thought and every moment are creation, so you must ask yourself, "Am I creating the intensity of desire to overcome the stuck places and ego tendencies?"

It is the ego's tendency to want to draw back from growth. With the ego's desire to stay in control, it chooses to hang back and not put itself totally into the effort. For so long in my life, I made efforts in the world, but I was halfway about it. Somewhere in my mind, I reasoned that if I did not put myself fully into the effort, and for some reason, it did not work out, I really didn't fail, because I had not put my full self into it. This may be true with many of you; you dabble at things. You do a little of this and a little of that, but you don't really get anywhere because you have not fully invested yourself.

There is an interesting phenomenon that I notice during most public lectures. When Mother spoke, I always wished to sit as close to her as possible, but in most situations, people will come to some lecture, perhaps after paying a lot of money for the privilege, then vie for the seats at the back of the room! The seats typically hardest to fill are the seats in the front. Why is that? The reason is: most people are reluctant to commit themselves. It is more comfortable to have one foot in the room, and the other next to the exit door.

This phenomenon of having one foot in and the other foot out, or at least close to the exit door, is common in the world. And it is the reason most do not get anywhere; their motives are mixed, their desires are mixed, and their emotions and thoughts are mixed. This is the single biggest reason for getting stuck on plateaus. People don't want to make a mistake, look foolish, to be thought poorly of by friends or family (or anybody for that matter). So, they stay in a "seasonless world," as Kahlil Gibran says, "where we laugh, but not all of our laughter, and cry, but not all of our tears."

It takes courage to commit to any venture a hundred percent. But unless you are willing to commit yourself, you will not gain the realization that will satisfy the soul. I think the great genius of Mother, Master, Papa, and the other great saints and realized masters is their clarity of purpose, thought, and feeling in committing themselves one hundred percent to the realization of God. For them, there was no sense of one foot in and the other next to a safety outlet. They were fully in the game. And that is the reason they succeeded in their quest. If you don't want to look foolish, if you are never willing to make a mistake, if you do not hold yourself responsible, then you will not reach the goal.

While leading this inner spiritual search, you must lead a balanced life; you can still do work in the world to support yourself and be a part of a family and social structure. But, as Sri Ramakrishna used to say, "When you work, keep one hand on God's foot and the other hand on your work. And when finished working, keep both hands on God's feet." Do you know what you will find when you do this? The inner communion with God, which is the rest and recuperation you have really been looking for. This is the true Sabbath day: you rest completely in your communion with omniscient consciousness when duties to the world are done.

Every day becomes a practice of letting go of attachments to the little and big things of life. Every day is a practice of orienting yourself to loving and serving God. Every day is a battlefield, destroying fear, greed, lust, moodiness, and dead inertia, and in turn winning victories of love, generosity, purity, and smooth temperament. Everyday life is your sadhana, the place where you surrender ego and are reborn in spiritual Self-hood. This is happening every day, every moment. And it is not tiring, although sometimes strenuous, and it is not defeating, although sometimes it can look overwhelming. Because when you are on the sadhanic battlefield, you are in the midst of life, and therefore life-energy. When you have Krishna as your charioteer, guide, friend, and your very Lord, then you can be assured of the battle won, no matter how dark things look. Know that always!

Throughout each day, you may assess at any moment, "Do I feel the Presence of God? Am I lessening my attachments to things of the world? Do I feel more loving and more in tune with selfless service now, today? Am I diving deeper into the ocean of God-Consciousness, into the peace, stillness, and all-pervading awareness?" No one day will look like another, and some days, despite your best efforts, the results will not seem to be what you would like them to be. But you can assess if you have made the "good fight." You do not control the results, but you do control the effort.

Therefore, keep your focus more on your efforts than the outcomes. The focus on your effort will tell more of the true story. And if you are making sincere efforts today, you will see results tomorrow. Break asunder all plateaus of inertia and negative tendencies with deepened prayer and meditation and know the Bliss that is the foundation for all creation! Know yourself to be one with that Bliss and be drawn up by the power of universal love into the all-embracing Union of Divine Consciousness. May it be ever so!

Om Sri Ram Jai Ram Jai Jai Ram

Becoming Poor in Spirit

"Blessed are they who are poor in spirit:
for theirs is the kingdom of heaven."
(Matthew 5:3)

Becoming poor in spirit means being dispassionate for the things of the world. Learning dispassion means being in a long process of learning, and relearning, all the ways we hang on to things of the body and the world. It has also been learning the means for releasing those attachments and letting them go.

In yogic thought, this dispassion is called vairagya. Unless one is an avadhoot, one who possesses nothing (not even a fig leaf), then we all have some possessions. The phrase *poor in spirit* means becoming *poor,* that is, detached or dispassionate about things of this body and possessions in the world, and *in spirit* means an inward renunciation, a mental and emotional letting go of attachment.

When the wealthy young man approached Jesus, saying he had followed all the commandments all his life, and asked what he needed to do to gain the kingdom of heaven, Jesus answered, "Sell everything, give it to the poor, and come, follow me." (Matthew 19:21 adapted) The man turned away sadly and walked away. And who today would make that choice? Who would sell everything in order to follow this command, *especially* if wealthy?

All of us have been born with a desire nature. In its simplest terms, desire nature is desire for happiness and cessation of pain. For one centered in body consciousness, that means comfort and security for the body with the least amount of threat. This can be sought in maximum body pleasure, a large bank account, a beautiful home, a prestigious job, power over others, world fame, etc.

For those of a spiritual bent, happiness means entering the kingdom of heaven and experiencing lasting Soul joy and peace, inner revelations of wisdom, and ultimate union with the Supreme

Consciousness. As we make spiritual progress, it becomes increasingly clear that preoccupation with things of the body and the world interferes with spiritual experience.

In order to make spiritual progress, there is a need to become less concerned with things of the world and increasingly focused on inward attunement with God. The problem in carrying out that shift of focus from the world to God comes to the fore, "I still live in the world; how do I participate in it but not be of it?"

What it comes down to is our mental perspective. A young boy was sent to a saint-king for instruction in spiritual matters. The boy had no faith in King Janaka and his spiritual instructions, as the trappings of wealth and power of the world surrounded him. The king started talking to the boy about living in the world but not being of it when a fire broke out in the palace where they were sitting. Attendants rushed to and from them with news of the fire. The king sat unconcerned, saying to the attendants he was busy talking about spiritual matters and he was sure they could take care of the fire. The king was so caught up in his talk about God, he would not even evacuate from the palace as the flames leapt near! At last, the boy's few spiritual books he had brought with him, his only possessions in the world, were being threatened by the flames. The boy was tamping out the sparks as they landed on his precious books. King Janaka commented, "Here I sit, totally focused on our discussion of God while this palace burns, yet you are distracted by your attachment to your books." The boy realized he had never seen the degree of vairagya, inner detachment, the king possessed. Humbled, he asked for pardon and earnestly requested initiation by the saint-king. Although outwardly a king, Janaka was inwardly *poor in spirit*.

Poor in spirit means to have the kind of inner detachment King Janaka demonstrated. When a fire destroyed a building at Anandashram, Swami Ramdas danced and laughed like a child watching the play of fire. Others were naturally upset that valuable property of the ashram was being destroyed. When news went out of the destruction of the building, new monies came; the old build-ing was replaced with a new and improved structure. Papa was ever calm, even delighted at the destruction of the old and the construc-tion of the new.

Everything of the world will pass. In one hundred years, with few exceptions, all the people now living on the earth will be dead. That is really an amazing thing when we think about it. We must realize that we rent, or at best we lease, our time here on earth; we are not buying! Yet, as I said before, we come with desires for happiness, and we have to maintain this body and any dependents we may have. How do we live in this world, take care of our body and our families, and yet remain detached? **One attitude is to see those desires we have in the world, for professional develop-ment, care of our family, etc., as coming from God. Let go of any sense of ownership of them.** As long as He puts the desire in our heart, let it be there by His will. If He chooses to withdraw the desire or to fulfill it, that is His doing. Inwardly, we are dispassion-ate witnesses.

If God chooses to create, build, or destroy through us, that is His doing. Be a pliant instrument for the Divine. Let the thrill of His expression run through our veins, yet hold no attachment for it to remain. He may choose to build a great empire through us; He may choose to remain inwardly withdrawn into our own Being with no outward activity; He may want to raise a family through us; He may want to be a dandy in us. **However He expresses Himself through us, let the focus of our attention be upon His absolute, change-less nature within us, and be a witness to how He chooses to express His creativity through us.** This requires our utmost sur-render and detachment.

How do we test whether we are detached or acting out of per-sonal motive? If detached, we will be able to stop any action at any moment and be carefree. With an inner command, we can walk away from everything and continue to reside in the pres-ence of God. Whether fame or blame presents itself, we are equally unaffected. If all possessions suddenly left us, we would feel equally Self-possessed. In short, we find our completeness and fulfillment through an inner wholeness that is independent of exterior conditions.

If we wonder if such Self-containment is possible, it is only because we have not experienced the absolute Consciousness that is God. Sadhana is made up of practicing detachment to the body and the world, but just as importantly, it is the positive attachment to the Presence of God. With that positive attachment, we find the things of the world are long on promises of happiness, but short on delivery. While God-experience takes initial effort to achieve but delivers far more than it demands.

We can begin detachment by inwardly and, if possible, outwardly simplifying our life. We fill our lives with so many things to do. With all the "time saving" devices we have in modern Western civilization, we would think that we would have excess time galore, but find it is quite the opposite. People feel more pressed for time than ever before. Why? Because with all that is available to us, that has quite literally not been available before, our expectations have grown even faster. We now believe that so much more should happen so much faster. The resolution? Simplify. To simplify, we must be willing to say no. We choose more carefully, more consciously, as to what we let into our lives.

One way to inwardly simplify is to practice going half speed. "Half speed?" you might say, "I won't get it all done!" But it is amazing, when slowing down, being fully present to what we are doing in this moment, we make fewer mistakes and things get done as well or better than when always being in a hurry, distracted, and pushing. It is confounding to our mind when tasks go smoother and are completed by moving at a Self-possessed speed. We can also practice slowing the mind down. Rather than thinking of ten things at once and by becoming inwardly calm and focused, while letting go of thoughts of other activities or of all the things that might go wrong, we bring Self-containment closer.

These activities that we surround ourselves with are addictive to the brain. The noise and activity of television, radio, going places, and always running from one place to another keeps us going at a faster pace. To *think* of slowing down feels so good, but instead, we add to the load. Why? Because underneath all the stress is a fear that if all this activity stopped, so would we. We would not have any place for all that stirred up energy to go and it would drive us crazy, kill us, make us a mess, or make us sick; in short, our world would fall apart. We have quite literally become addicted to all the stimulation. This is the way of rajasic, stimulating energy.

To compensate for all this stimulation, we alternate it with trying to over-satiate the body. Through food, sex, sleep, and activities aimed at calming all that energy, we seek to find some peace. Through overdoing satiating activities, including alcohol and drugs, we hope to find relief for our overstimulated nerves. This is the tamasic, negative state leading to an unconscious stupor. Such mediums as television can be rajasic, passive stimulation to the nerves, such as the excitement of a sporting event, or tamasic, mind-numbing "vegging out."

For many people, one or both of these states of rajasic and tamasic is all that life is. Even a religious life can be just one more meeting to go to, another activity in joining the choir, being on the board of directors, teaching Sunday school, or perhaps a place to get that perfect nap during the sermon! In reality, these are not all that different in quality from the rest of our life.

A quality resides beyond the active rajasic and the numbing tamasic. This third state may be all too fleeting and rare in our life. It is the sattvic, uplifted, state of being. When in a sattvic state, we have spontaneously occurring joy and peace. It comes to us not by worldly activity or satiation of the senses, but through a flow from an inner source. "Sounds perfect," says the overly stimulated/satiated individual. But there is a catch. "Oh, I knew it, nothing comes for free!" says the rajasic merchant-thinker. We must learn to be still. "What, and waste my time doing nothing? What for? Can't I join a club or something and get it through activity?" says the activist. Well, yes, we can learn to be outwardly active but inwardly still. But first, **we must learn to be still.** A terrifying thought for many.

Let someone addicted to activity and satiated senses try meditating quietly for five minutes. "Well, that's it, time must be over. On to do some things I've just got to get done!" says rajasic thinkers after their allotted five minutes. Or the tamasic thinker says, "That was a quick five-minute nap, maybe I can get another half-hour nap before I get going!" Letting go of rajasic and tamasic states is another level of what it means to become *poor in spirit*. One renounces attachment to constant doing and satiation. No small task for those addicted to these twins. But, in order to enter the inner kingdom of heaven, this is the key: to become dispassionate towards things of the senses and things of the world, including the tamasic and rajasic states.

For such a one who willingly practices inner dispassion for the world and focuses on the positive attraction to the Spirit, an inner world of realization awaits. Currently, that Spirit may be slumbering, or at least partially slumbering, within us. But with outwardly slowing down, simplifying, practicing inner renunciation, and having repeated contact with Spiritual Consciousness we begin to change—with new eyes, we see the outer things of the world to be God's play. The inner states of Spiritual Consciousness are seen to be the transcendent Reality of lasting joy. No longer addicted to stimulations of the world, and no longer seeing the world as a source of our ultimate fulfillment, we live from the *inside-out,* instead of the *outside-in.* Living from the *outside-in* means things of the world and the senses are the primary focus for happiness and fulfillment and dictate our direction in life. Living from the *inside-out* means spiritual attunement is our source of happiness and fulfillment and direction in life comes from intuition that guides outward actions.

Through the inner dissection of outer attachments with the scalpel of wisdom, our minds become steady and are able to focus on inner stillness. The rajasic-tamasic twins come into their subservient roles as designed. Having become *poor in spirit* to the world, we enter into that inner kingdom of heaven, a mansion with many rooms. We explore the vast potential of who we are in Spirit. With the lower forces mastered, we participate in the world, but we are not of it. New hope for new men and women! True men and true women of a new age, finding fulfillment within and expressing it in all they do. May it come to be, even now!

A World Stood on Its Head

O Lord, I have had wealth
It bought me only misery with fleeting happiness.
I have had possessions, the best the world had to offer
Each was a burden on my back.
I had world authority, even unto life and death
Each decision ladened me with terrible responsibility.
I waged war and gained immense power
And it became an anchor to my soul.

And now, I have no material wealth
And possess immeasurable happiness.
I own little, and would happily relieve myself of that
And I feel the lightness of Being.
I have no authority in the world
But there are those who would lay down their lives for mine.
I now wage war on ignorance and wish all to have peace
And my soul is set free.

Spirit has turned the world on its head
Those things I thought would bring pleasure, brought pain instead.
Power that brought fame
Resulted in disturbance and disaster
Use of force made me a prisoner.
O Lord, free me of worldly gain
Make me poor in spirit
So I may be rich in You.

The Washerman—Washerwoman

Sadhana may be compared to washing clothes by hand. One begins with soiled clothes. Some detergent is applied and the rough work of squeezing, hitting, and pressing the clothes, along with some vigorous rubbing, brings the soil out and makes the clothes clean again. The clothes are then hung to dry in the sun.

The mind full of worldly desires and attachments is the soiled cloth. Detergent added is the grace of the guru. Squeezing the clothes is applying the directions of the guru, hitting is the use of one's own will, pressing is devotion of the heart, and the vigorous rubbing is the interactions in the world for sadhana's sake.

Even with the application of all the above, there may be stains left that seem part of the fabric itself. It is the Grace of God Himself that alone can remove these stains through complete surrender by the sadhaka. So, it is through following the directions of the guru, application of one's will, working in the world to resolve one's own karma, and by Grace of God and Gurus that one may be freed of a soiled mind and stand free in the pure sunshine light of God.

Sadhakas go to the Movies

Going to watch a film for a sadhaka is a test. The whole intent of the makers of the movie is to "pull you in" to the story line. Whether to make you laugh, cry, or tighten in fear, they wish you to identify with the characters in the film, in order to move you in some way. If the movie-goer gets involved with the storyline, they will find themselves laughing, crying, or in total fright. And, at what? Nothing but a play of light on a screen and some sound. Still, that play of light can evoke all the emotions and even sensations of physical world experiences. This proves that attachment to the word is mental.

If sadhakas can go to the movies, be in the movies but not of them, then they may have all the enjoyment of the movie but not be lost in the movie, that is, to forget who they really are. Laughter may be there, even some tears and fright, but not all the way. Always, inside, they keep some portion of themselves inviolate, pure, without identification with reactions to the play. That way, they stay aware of their greater reality and know it is just a play.

When you live life this way, in and out of the movie house, and know that you are really God playing a part in the vast drama of life, then you are free, even within the play itself.

Know a Gift's Value

Seekers of Truth, in meeting, and many who are initiated by a true Teacher-Guru are likened to children of a very wealthy father. The father lavishes gifts upon the children. He willingly gives them gives gifts of gold bonds, blue chip stocks, and silver certificates. Unknowingly and foolishly, the children redeem these treasures for things of little value. With unseeing eyes, they look upon these gifts, not comprehending their true worth. They go to the corner market and seeing shiny trinkets for sale, they dream of having some of those things. So, they consign themselves to the merchant, live in the merchant's basement, and abandon their father who loves them so. The father waits and waits with longing for their return, but they return not. Thinking only of their trinkets, they let languish their treasures unused or spent for foolish trinkets.

O Sadhakas, count not yourselves among those foolish ones who have eyes but do not see, and who have ears but do not hear. The eventide of this life comes nigh too soon. Let not your gifted treasure be for naught. For you are accountable for all things. And if you but bury that treasure, then like the man or woman of one talent, even that which was given is taken away. See that you are like the person given five talents, doubling their value, and therefore proving your worth to be given even more. (Matthew 25:14–30)

O Sadhakas, be like that one, and ye shall be inheritors of your Father in Heaven's vast wealth. Invest what you have been given into time, effort, and intensity, and your return will be realized many times over.

Be an Instrument of Joy

The Sadhana of service is not done for any particular outcome. No matter how sincerely we believe what we are doing is essential or doing a good, that good or need we are fulfilling could be wiped out in a moment. Then, one might ask, why act? We act because ultimately it is God moving through us in that action. Even in fulfilling so-called mundane desires of eating, providing shelter, or clothing ourselves, it is Divinity Itself that moves through us, as the creative idea, the energy in the doing, and the material/physical creation of all action. The Power and Intelligence flowing to us make us creative, give us energy, and manifest physical creation.

I am sure that people thousands of years ago performed actions they believed to be good or essential, but who remembers them now? To act as an instrument of the Divine means we become the observers of how Divine Intelligence directs us, how life-energy moves through our bodies, and how the material/physical aspect comes together. Through purification of the mind, we attune ourselves to the essence of Spirit in action. We feel the purity, the joy, the fulfillment in being the instrument. Just as a musical instrument, such as a flute, does not play its own music, but rather the musician plays its music through the flute, even so, we are the instruments of the Divine.

We play for the joy of being played. The more we surrender our individual will to the Divine Will, the more we become perfect instruments for Spiritual expression. Stubborn individual will is like keys of the flute that stick or become frozen. Pride and jealousy likewise make the instrument partially or totally unusable for sacred use. Making ourselves soft and pliable, sensitive to the most subtle of movements, we will be an instrument the master musician will find joy in playing; all who hear the instrument will find joy in listening, and the instrument itself will be in joy just due to the fact it is being played by the master.

Guru

Guru is in your heart. Guru is the glorious Light of God. Guru is sown into every part of creation. Guru is savior of mankind. Through the Light of Guru, darkness is dispelled. Guru is universal, without beginning or end. See the blazing Light of the Guru! Know ye not you are made in Its likeness of Spirit and It inhabits your image of the three bodies. Guru is love. Guru is Light. Guru is wisdom. Guru is power of Yoga. Guru is not man, woman, nor any one person or thing. Guru is savior to all creation. Guru uses man, woman, or any vehicle It chooses to transform souls darkened in ignorance into enlightened Souls of Realization. As loving as mother and father is the Guru. As desirous for union as newlywed couples is Guru to be in union with their beloved devotees. Union not of bodies, but of hearts, minds, and souls. Union to Universal Consciousness. A union to the Union of all unions. O glorious and ecstatic Guru! In form or formlessness, It burns ever within you and all about you. O sadhaka, purify your eyes so you may see Its glory. Make your eye of attention single so you may see Its Light. Quiet the mind so you may hear its entrancing voice. It is nigh to you now. Wait no longer but find your Guru now, now ever now! (Written in an ecstatic moment.)

Inner Renunciation

John the Baptist is the forerunner of Jesus and preaches, "Repent ye: for the kingdom of heaven is at hand." (Matthew 3:2) To repent means to turn away from, to renounce. This spirit of John the Baptist comes upon us and induces a spirit of renunciation from within. John lived outside of the cities of men; his clothes were not fine, his food sparse and wild. His was the life of a renunciate. As we know, it must be an inner life of renunciation, as outer acts do not necessarily correspond to the inner nature. John is the forerunner to the Christ, the Messiah. That is to say, before Christ Consciousness can come, a spirit of renunciation must be present.

Before Mother Hamilton started the inner Mystical Crucifixion, she and her husband sold all that they had in order to go to India. Both she and her husband were in their mid-fifties, a time of life when most people are very serious about retirement, pensions, the equity in their home, etc. Mother and her husband, Ralph, sold all to make the trip to India! When arriving at Anandashram, Swami Ramdas made it clear every attachment had to be renounced, thrown into the ocean of God. Mother had a fierce love of her children. With all her heart, she renounced special attachment to her husband and children. All this is in the spirit of John the Baptist, as a voice calling in the wilderness. The wilderness is a state of mind when the sadhaka realizes the things of the world will not bring fulfillment. Inwardly, the sadhaka has left the "cities of men," those attachments to worldly aspirations, but one has yet to enter the holy city of consciousness, so remains in the wilderness. The voice of one crying is the voice of intuition that tells it is time to let go of the things of this world, but that voice is not yet the Christ Consciousness; it is the forerunner of it.

In this spirit of renunciation, some aspirants get attached to the world of non-attachment. Becoming prideful in their ability to do without, they do not proceed further. Some of John the Baptist's disciples did not go on to follow Jesus because he was not following an outer life of renunciation as John, their teacher, did. Also, in the Buddha's case, there were those who practiced with him the outer austerities during the seven years he made those his sadhana. When he left that path of severe outer renunciation for the middle path, they did not go with him.

As mentioned, the spirit of renunciation is an inner one. Jesus' very first recorded saying in the Sermon on the Mount is, "Blessed are the poor in spirit, for theirs is the kingdom of heaven." (Matthew 5:3) To be poor of course meant to own nothing, and in spirit means inwardly. So, to be poor in spirit means to have inwardly renounced the world, body consciousness; the kingdom of heaven, Spiritual Consciousness, becomes your state of Being. Krishna, in the Bhagavad Gita, says it this way, "He who is unattached to everything, and meeting with good and evil, neither rejoices nor recoils, his mind is stable... The self-controlled Sadhaka (disciple) while enjoying the varying sense-objects through his senses, which are disciplined from likes and dislikes, attains placidity of mind. With the attainment of such placidity of mind, all his sorrows come to an end; and the intellect of such a person of tranquil mind soon withdrawing itself from all sides, becomes firmly established in God." (Gita 2:57)

The attainment of this inner renunciation is the heart and soul of Sadhana at this stage. In Jnana Yoga, the mind uses the sword of discrimination to cut out all attachments. The mind is in constant vigil; no attachment is allowed to reside in the mind. In Raja Yoga, renunciation is practiced through pranayama, life-force control, to draw all life-force, normally channeled into sense consciousness, back into the spinal nervous system up into higher Consciousness. John the Baptist was in the River Jordan where he washed sins away. The River Jordan inwardly represents the spinal nervous system. When, through the spirit of inner renunciation, life-force is drawn into the spine and lifted upwards, the sin of separation from God is washed away in the holy vibration felt there. The third Yoga is Bhakti. Through intense love and devotion for God, the mind is turned inward to attain union with the Beloved. And, in the fourth Yoga, Karma, all activities are dedicated to the service of God. Eventually, one feels that it is God Himself who is doing the work, and with this, the mind is turned inwards even while engaged in outer activities. All four Yogas lead to the same goal—an inward mind. Detached from the ups and downs of worldly events, the steady mind feels its union with the Sat Chid Ananda nature of God. The establishment of the individual consciousness of the soul in this all-embracing Consciousness of God is the kingdom of heaven.

In East and West, the message is the same. A renunciation of worldly consciousness and turning the mind inward reveals a Kingdom of Spirit residing within every soul. When the inner eye of Spirit is opened, it reveals that same Light, that same Spirit found within is also saturating all creation. Like people with closed eyes, once having opened their eyes see sunlight all around. At once they realize their darkness was self-induced. Before, when their eyes were closed, they would say to one and all, "The world is so dark!" Now they proclaim to all who still have closed eyes, "Open your eyes; there is light all about you." But something keeps those with closed eyes from opening them. They remain in their blindness. Such is the nature of world-bound souls.

In order to enter Spiritual Realms of Light, we must become inner renunciants to world darkness, to become poor in spirit. Then, through making the mind inward through Jnana, Raja, Bhakti, and/ or Karma Yogas, we attain to God Supreme. Let us listen for the voice of one crying in the wilderness, the voice of one leading us the way to Christ Consciousness, to "Repent ye: for the kingdom of heaven is at hand."

Kundalini

Many years ago, I sat in meditation pose as a part of a group in Bellingham, Washington, intent upon the kutastha chaitanya, the third eye point. Twenty-four years ago in the fall of 1976, I had been a student/disciple of Mother Hamilton for one and a half years. I came with a burning desire for God, although I would not have put those words to it when I first came to Mother. She redeemed the word "God" for me in my mind and gave me a living teaching for Who and What He is. Mother taught me that by meditating upon the point between the eyebrows, God might reveal Himself.

All of a sudden, as I meditated in that group, a "snap" was felt and inwardly heard. With that snap, an upward surge of energy directly and powerfully rose up my spine and curved from the lower part of my skull at the medulla, and shot across to the third eye point upon which I was meditating! In this sudden dramatic movement, I was a helpless onlooker. The energy at the ajna created a terrific heat. Fortunately, I had been grounded in Mother's teachings and knew of this force, though nothing can truly prepare you for it.

The heat became intense. The thought came to me, "I could fry eggs on my forehead!" Strange thought, but there you have it. I knew not what to do but to keep my attention on this spot. In fact, there was nothing else I could have done. Like a powerful magnet, it drew my whole awareness to this area, along with the feeling of power that was surging up my spine. The body was in the background of my awareness, but demanded no attention. It is difficult to gauge time in these matters, but I would guess for ten or fifteen minutes this powerful surge of kundalini continued unabated.

Slowly, the force subsided. I did not know whether to be sorry or glad. I was so grateful for this mystical experience, but a bit overwhelmed by its power, and the body felt it had been terrifically strained. Still, I wanted more. I wanted realization of the Self and was willing to do whatever I needed to achieve it.

Twenty-four years later, today, I can say that enthusiasm for this path and the realization it brings has not subsided in the least. As Yogananda's song extols, "Devotees may come, devotees may go, devotes may come, devotees may go, but my Lord, I will Love Thee always, my Lord, I will love Thee always." So as with the song, so with the devotee.

Earlier today at the Cloud Mountain Retreat Center, I was meditating in front of a shrine that is here in the cabin with a figure in it. The figure's lower part of the body is a serpent, the upper half, a woman's winged figure. Above her head, the heads of five serpents. The woman sits serene. Apparently, this goddess has its own traditions and meanings in Buddhism. But in my mind, I see her as kundalini shakti risen in full self-mastery of the lower five chakras and fully residing in the sixth chakra, or the realm of the realized Buddha, Christ, or Krishna Consciousness. "And as Moses lifted up the serpent in wilderness, even so must the son of man be lifted up." (John 3:14) Any attempt to be in a fully illumined state without the complete illumination of the ego is an unrighteous way and will result in boomerang karmic results.

As I prayed to God in the form of this goddess, memories flitted across my mental screen. Memories of my path since that first awakening. A sense of, well, not exactly regret, but a longing, a yearning deep down that I could have had a purer, more refined, more mature understanding during those years. I struggled, I did the best I could, and have somehow lived through it all. I had the perfect teacher and example in my Guru. This alone I am sure is what has made it possible to be where I am now.

But, this yearning to have been different, better, reminds me of a favorite story. The chief of a tribe approached a father and said, "It is time for your son to join the hunt." The father responded, "Yes, I have been thinking the same thing. Shall he be part of the next hunting party?" "Yes," answered the chief, and so it was agreed.

Now the father started thinking about the hunts. They were sometimes long, dangerous journeys that required physical endurance and mental stamina. Then he reflected on his son, not fully physically mature, sometimes like a little boy in behavior. He went to the chief and told him that he, the father, didn't think his son was ready for the hunt. The chief started chuckling, hardly containing himself. He saw straight to the heart of the issue. The chief, when he recovered himself, said, "Of course your son is not ready for the hunt; the hunt will make him ready for the hunt!"

Well, this is the spiritual path in a nutshell! We do not begin at the end. We must begin exactly where we are at, not at some idealized picture of ourselves that may not have any truth in it anyway. We begin with the rough stuff of what we are. We have aspirations, dreams, hopes, strengths, ideals, etc., all on the plus side. On the shady side of the street are our fears, angers, unresolved past issues, inadequacies, weaknesses—shall I go on? Get the picture? This is us. This is a snapshot of us at that moment. No getting around it, no denying it, or at least no good reason to deny it. Why do I mention all of this in relation to the kundalini?

Because the kundalini is all about purifying the very stuff of what we are made of. Jesus said the sheep that are on the right get in, the goats on the left are out! (Matthew 25:32–33) Now he's not talking about people, even if we think we know a few goats. He is referring to the individual. We are all made of mixed character. Can't be helped, that's how it is. But don't despair, and don't rest satisfied—proceed with patient expectation.

Now, kundalini is a response to an intense soul desire. (If you think the kundalini has not been awakened in you, you may be right, and this is a call to intensify sadhana.) But kundalini is not realization by itself, it is a necessary means to gain realization. Realization is a result of the purification of the mind. Purification of the mind comes from keeping the mind on God at all times. This focused attention comes through meditation, prayer, chanting, serving, and loving God.

Through this intense focus of attention on God, the kundalini is activated and purifies and strengthens the nerve pathways of the physical and astral bodies. It also awakens higher centers of Consciousness within the sadhaka. **But, unless the purification of the mind, through a singular focus on God, accompanies that kundalini action, the kundalini energy will be dissipated or will run in unnatural avenues.** If the kundalini is dissipated or misdirected it will not achieve its ultimate purpose: conscious Self-realization.

Some sadhakas will have a sudden or powerful experience of the kundalini and through fear will shut the transformation power off. Even as this intelligent force will guide and direct us, so will it respond to our strong will. Whatever is on the conscious or sub-conscious mind will be strengthened by this force. An ego-driven person may become even more so, and consequently misuse the energy. Others will have surface or latent desire nature activated. The energy channeled through sex nerves, desire for name, fame, wealth, power, and control can subvert purity of spiritual purpose.

And what is purity of mind? It is a total, one-hundred-per-cent, surrender to the Infinite. It is the realization, even as Jesus had, "Of myself I am nothing, it is my Father who doeth the works." (John 14:10 adapted) Purity of mind is surrendering to the highest inner workings of the kundalini shakti in order to scale the summit of Realization. And through this action, the old self, the ego, is dead and the resurrected Self, the Christ Consciousness, lives.

The inner fulfillment of the world's great scriptures requires this individual purity of purpose by the sadhaka. Those that would try to enter by "some other way" other than surrender of the ego will not attain their purpose. (John 10:1) The law must be fulfilled; the price must be paid. And those who choose not to pay the price should not be pretenders to the throne. Jesus' worst pronouncements were on those religious leaders who perverted their office for personal gain of name, fame, and fulfillment of ego gratification. Woe be unto them! (Matthew 23:13) For their penalty of karmic debt is much greater for this hypocrisy than any other. All who would enter must pass through the steep path and narrow gate. (Matthew 7:13–14)

And, if we are willing to lay down our lives, perhaps literally, in obeyance of this requirement for purity? What then? Then the kundalini will go about its high purpose. This means the purification of the body temple, a body made new in Christ. It means the kundalini will enter the seven inner churches and light the seven inner candles of Supreme Consciousness. (Revelation 1:20) The work of resolving the knots of past karma ensues from our conscious and subconscious minds in order to gain in purity of mind.

Latent tendencies are exposed in order to cast them into the purifying flame of Light. And if instead of casting them in the fires, we act on these desires, reigniting their dormant life-force? Then we find ourselves in a battle royal for supremacy within the consciousness. Each positive attention paid to past desires feeds the spark with the rocket fuel of kundalini. If we give in to this tendency, the mind will find justification for its action. It will reason: this fulfillment of desire is why I was born; I cannot live without that desire; things spiritual are false, a passing phase, for someone else but not for me, etc. The mind will find every possible trick to tempt us to go with the triggered desire. Why? Because that is the nature of desire, to fulfill itself. It takes no account of the cost to ourselves or others.

And what of that one who chooses this? They wander the path of self-justification. They deride spiritual law as antiquated. Some others perhaps feel that they have risen above such laws as the Ten Commandments. But Jesus said the God-man comes to fulfill the law, not destroy it. (Matthew 5:17) The mind is ruthless in its attempts to have its own way, though. Gradually, usually not all at once, that one loses their light and falls back into the ignorance of separation from God. Sadly, an opportunity is lost. The kundalini either retires back to dormancy or is manipulated into wrongful purpose.

The other possibility is they awaken to their error. Realizing they have made poor choices, they humbly retrace the steep trail back to their wrong turn. They make amends where possible, repent, or turn away from their error and get started back on the path to enlightenment.

I have known a good many souls seduced into subverting their experiences through wrong desire. In some cases, it resulted in death, in most it resulted in strong accusations against a moral path and the spiritual teacher. In some, a more moderate denial of their Spiritual Nature, substituting psychic phenomena that enhances ego, instead of the ego-annihilating spiritual path. In either case, the ultimate destiny of the soul will be fulfilled: that is, the consummation of the separated ego-self into the all-embracing God-self. In this lifetime, or in some other, the soul will once again awaken to its desire for ultimate realization. We may each wisely take from these examples the lesson that even for highly realized souls, the journey to Self is fraught with pitfalls. Unless we cultivate that pure desire for the complete realization of Self, we may very well suffer similar fates.

Karma and Kundalini

Karma is a result of our free will, revocable—never. There is no arbitrary God casting out judgments in anger or jealousy. There is nothing more difficult than the law of karma, the law of cause and effect. Mathematical in efficiency, it is the cosmic feedback machine that lets us experience the impact of all our thoughts, words, and actions. That is why to love God and all creation as yourself is not just a sentimental abstraction. It puts into effect a very exacting law. What you give, you receive.

There is the joke, "Why did God create time?" Pause... "So everything doesn't happen at once!" Well, in the realm of karma, not every effect comes immediately after its cause. There is a time lag and a build-up time. Individuals with very good metabolic health may have to work a lifetime to destroy the good health karma with which they were born. So, the full effect of past actions, good or bad, may take time to manifest. As we might imagine, karma is a complex weave of mixed patterns.

When we say to the universe, "I am ready to go to my spiritual home now," with pure intention, the operating Intelligence of all that is sets into motion all the conditions that are necessary for that desire to be fulfilled. That means meeting and resolving our past actions. "For verily I say unto you, Till heaven and earth pass, not one jot or one tittle shall in no wise pass from the law, till all be fulfilled." (Matthew 5:18) Like people who collected credit cards like baseball cards and use them to their maximum, there comes a day when the bill is due. All resources are then applied to paying previous debt, sometimes just enough to survive on now is used for present living. The sadhaka may complain, "My life seemed better before I set myself on this path!" Just as the credit card holder can say life before paying off this debt was "easy street."

But in all of this payment of debt, there is help. Just as those in credit trouble may go to an agency that takes over their finances and arranges all payments, so may sadhakas cast all the burden of the debt upon God. Now, if the credit-troubled man or woman gets help but secretly gets more credit and uses it, he or she breaks the agreement, and help is withdrawn. So, with God. But, if the sadhaka is sincere, then God truly lifts the burden and makes the load light. All we have to concern ourselves with is attunement with God in this moment and feel His Presence, unconditional love, and guidance.

The guru also is there to take the load. As the credit-troubled man or woman may win the sympathy of a wealthy individual, especially if the rich person sees the burdened individual really struggling to do the right thing, so the guru lifts burdens from the sadhaka.

One of the things Jesus got into hot water for was when he said, "Thy sins are forgiven you." (Matthew 9:2) Those who went by the law decried that as blasphemy. No one can forgive sins. But Jesus was a living testament to the fact that a human being can be one with the omniscient Spirit of our heavenly Father.

Through God-tuned thought, the God-man may project an idea that purifies the sadhaka from a darkened blot of the past, or take onto his or her own body the effect of some past actions of the sadhaka. Such is the grace of God acting through the God-man or God-woman. And Jesus came to show what was possible for all who would pick up their cross, their body, and follow him, the God-tuned life of complete surrender.[18] This all occurs for the purification effect that kundalini energy is creating in the sadhaka.

There is great comfort for sadhakas when they know that each knock received is another debt paid. Let purification proceed! We do not need to seek out trouble or pain in some vain attempt to pay off karma! For that would truly be vanity. Difficulties, if they are to come, can find their way to our door without our help. Rather than fixate on what debt there might be, let us get busy with liberating the mind now. Whatever comes our way, with God-thoughts centered in the mind, bliss, joy, love, and freedom are ours now! Let the body go through what it must, if it is to be. But we may know our oneness now by letting the mind be intermingled with the ever-present Christ Light within us. Such is the grace being offered. The father of the prodigal son ran out to greet him when he was a

---

18   Jesus referred to the cross long before the crucifixion: "Then said Jesus unto his disciples, If any man will come after me, let him deny himself, and take up his cross, and follow me." (Matthew 16:24)

long way off, to make his peace with him. We may also know that peace now.

We do not know where we are, how near or far. Some sadhakas may have had experiences we've not had. But that may be because we have already gone through them in another lifetime. Do not compare—only look to that singular Light of Being and harmonize ourselves with that Essence. All else will be taken care of perfectly.

As I mentioned before, kundalini may come in dramatic ways or more subtle ways. Do not try to judge such things. Let us focus our mind on whether we are experiencing oneness with the all-embracing Spirit. We will know that through expanding, ever-new joy, a sure knowledge that we and our Father are one. We will feel ourselves to be an instrument or an expression of God in action through service, and will feel universal love and compassion for all. These are the signs of oneness with God. These are the rooms of our inner Kingdom. When we have this purity of experience, without a second, as our natural way of Being, then God will confirm for us our oneness with Him.

Until then, more sadhana! That is to keep the mind firmly fixed on God, to allow Him to arrange all for our progress and purify our lower desire nature into transmuted Divine Nature.

Jai Shakti Kundalini, Jai Guru, Jai Ram

The String of Intuition

How do we know what our intuition is telling us? This question often comes up when speaking of following our inner knowing. It is both a subject that we can apply too much, and too little, thought to. This may sound like a strange contradiction, but let us reason it through together. If we apply too much thought to the field of intuition, then we will block our intuition. If we apply too little thought, then we will accept every passing thought and fancy for being true intuition. We must train ourselves to be both open to intuitive thought, and be willing to "Test every spirit." (1 John 4:1)

The essential ingredient for developing intuitive thought is to learn to be still, to quiet the body, emotions, and thoughts that normally occupy our everyday experience. In that stillness, a certain kind of knowing may come to us. It comes initially as "a still, small voice." We may feel it as a tug in a direction in our lives, or suddenly we come to know the rightness of going in a certain direction. It may come as a whole or complete picture of everything that is to occur, or we sense what our next step ought to be. In either case, following our intuition means taking the next step toward our ultimate goal. This movement is like picking up the end of a string and following it. It takes a certain amount of faith to do this: faith in inner knowing, faith in ourselves. Intuition coming as that inner knowing may stem from the mind's ability to unconsciously assimilate information, or to recognize patterns that present us with solutions. Or, that inner knowing may be the ability of our consciousness to reach beyond normal ways of thinking, giving us access to the psychic realm or the Superconscious realm.

Through intuition, we have information not derived through a sequential, reasoned thought process. We may test that knowing in several different ways—some using reason and intuition. Some reasoning ways of testing what we are getting is to ask, "Is this for a positive purpose for myself, my family, my community?" Also, "Will this be for the highest good of everyone concerned?" Thirdly, "Does it make common sense, or at least, can I see a logical sequence of events that will lead to a good?" If we can answer affirmatively to these questions, then we may feel we are on safer ground. In relation to the third question, intuition may outdistance the reasoning mind's ability to pull in all the rational information to know if it makes logical sense. Therefore, we may not be able to answer this question fully.

Intuitive confirmation can be sought by asking for a response from our intuitive felt-sense. For instance, we can ask, "Does this measure up to the highest Light of which I am capable of knowing right now?" Or, if we ask God, "Is this a true intuition of Your will?" When asking these questions, it is important to become still, clearing the mind and body of the flow of thoughts and feelings and to listen for the voice of God—that higher means of knowing from the Superconscious. From that stillness, is there a positive response? Ultimately, we can only be certain of what may be intended for us in the moment. Other confirmations may come by asking a fully realized Being, or if time proves the intuition as coming true, then it becomes a prophecy fulfilled.

When we first get an inner prompting and continue to follow that voice of intuition, we have picked up the end of the string and we are following it. That is, we respond to what we are getting intuitively in each moment. Then we continue on to each next step, all the while testing the intuitive prompts, both cognitively and intuitively. We may not know the whole of our journey, but we will always know the next step. And, if nothing comes to us? We then check, are we still in our feelings, and are our thoughts open to what may come? If the inner stillness reveals no prompting for action, then the direction is to not act. However, we stay alert, open for the next movement to action. It is by following each step in this way that will keep us focused on the moment and support our making progress toward the ultimate goal. It also keeps us focused on that inner Light and helps us to fulfill our Dharma—the reason we are here. **This method requires faith, a faith that replaces a need to know all the details of a journey before we take a single step.**

One example comes to mind of being guided by this inner knowingness. Once I was in a large department store. I had been shopping while a friend had gone to another part of the store; where, I did not know. I was done shopping and wanted to find my friend. I felt a magnetic force guide my movements up an escalator and then another. I felt my steps guided while in the grip of this magnetic force. I was made to turn in circles at times for no apparent reason. I had to suspend my resistance to being noticed by others for some strange movements on my part and release myself to this guiding force. Finally, I was made to stand in a certain place on the third floor and then to stare in one direction. The magnetic force kept me standing there. I wondered why I was staring at a part of the store that was empty of all persons, when my friend stepped out of a dressing room at that very moment!

Now, clearly, the force that guided me was more than anything I could have known through the five senses. As a receiver of this information, it was required that I open myself to such guidance through a calm, receptive mind. Second, that I be willing to overcome my self-consciousness relative to what others would think of me so I could stay attuned to this inner direction. Third, that I surrender to this inner prompting without knowing the final outcome before starting. Other cases of intuition may be more or less dramatic than this example.

Every day, intuition may come in seemingly very ordinary ways. We may be wondering what to do next in life. When asking this very big question about our life, no direct answer comes. An inner prompting suddenly comes to clean the bathroom! Now, what does that have to do with one's life's purpose? In this case, it can be picking up the end of the string and starting the journey. Getting our house in order may be the first step in getting onto our life's purpose. And so, we clean the bathroom. While cleaning, an idea comes into our mind about a book we once read and were inspired by at the time. Following the string, we find that book and open it at random. We read how the hero was inspired to do what he or she loved to do, following the greatest Light. It comes to us that we have followed a route of least resistance and have lost touch with that inner knowing of what we always wanted to do. Fear grips us. We ask, "Can I do that? Do I continue to follow the string, or do I let the fear stop me?"

Emotions such as fear and anger block our inner knowing. Also, desire nature such as greed and lust will overshadow intuition. That is why out-of-control emotions and desire nature are so destructive to making good decisions in attunement with our inner direction. The practice of meditation, quieting the mind through focused attention, teaches us to remain the observer of our thoughts and feelings, not denying or identifying with them. Free of distracting thoughts and feelings, we become aware of that still, small voice of intuition.

As we increasingly value being guided by intuition, then our receptivity increases. Grand visions of what can be may stretch out before our inner vision. Even with these grand vistas must come the steps to gaining these vistas. By honoring this inner stillness and gaining the rich harvest of inspiration and Divine direction, our life is founded upon the hard rock of realization of that kingdom of Light. May we all come to grasp firmly that string of intuition that leads us to fulfill our life's purpose and further bring the fruits of that kingdom of Light, both within and without.

Meditation as Renunciation

The sadhaka gains strength from acts of renunciation. Renunciation may be thought of as any turning away from the world and focusing on God. Turning away from the world means turning away from the sensory stimulations and striving nature of desire for things of this world.

One of the greatest extremes of renunciation is meditation. In meditation, we close the eyes; we are in a quiet place; we are in a relaxed posture without touching or being or being touched; we have the mouth closed and we are not actively smelling our environment. All five senses are brought to a quiet standstill.

Next, the mind, which runs after things of the world, past, present, and future, that active mind with its constant commentary on everything, hopping all over the place, is slowly trained to become still. Either we learn to be the observer, the stillness behind the thoughts, or we learn to become one-pointed in our focus. Either way, the mind becomes still, and we renounce thoughts of this world.

Having renounced the senses and thoughts, and having come to a stillness, we make ourselves attentive, but without desire. This means we also renounce desire for enlightenment or any spiritual experience. This is the final stage of the renunciate.

Complete renunciation leads to enlightenment. Enlightenment answers all the questions, whose answers we have sought in running after the things of the senses and the world.

With the senses restrained, mind focused on the Supreme Lord of the Universe, and empty of desire, we are the complete renunciate. Anytime we imitate this complete renunciation of the outer by replacing it through some inner act, we can help prepare ourselves for that complete inner renunciation.

Our attempts at meditation are ways to imitate complete inner renunciation. Even though the attempt to meditate is not successful, it will yield results. We may struggle through the entire time we sit for meditation. The senses scream for attention, the mind runs like a herd of wild horses, and we are in painful agony or utter restlessness the whole time. We are completely relieved to be done with our sitting time and leave our asana like a racehorse leaving the starting gate!

Yet strangely enough, the after-effect of our time in meditation is quite wonderful. Either immediately after, or later in the day, we feel purified, at peace, and very centered; the complete opposite, but hoped for, experience in meditation. The mind wonders if the meditation was a waste of time, yet we feel this way afterward. The stringency of the meditation is directly responsible for the uplifted mood, later on.

The difference in how we get to sensory satisfaction and spiritual satisfaction can be compared to how we earn and spend money. Sensory satisfaction is like getting a credit card and running up the bill, paying only the minimum amount due. The fun is all up front, with an increasing debt load, added to by the accumulating interest charges. Whatever is purchased in this way costs many times the original amount.

By working and saving, however, the most difficult part is done first, and the savings compared to the credit method is really significant. When we "spend" our life-energy on the senses first, we accumulate a debt. By investing in the body and the world all of our life-energy, we forget our Divine origins. This forgetfulness results in a huge expenditure on the body and world that: 1) will go away all too soon, and 2) leaves us spiritually bankrupt when we leave this body.

Attending church once a week will not balance this account. Leaving this body with a huge "amount owing" to this world requires we come again to work out the balance. At least if we live a moral life, we will not be so much in the red, but God help us if we fudge the numbers or were outright corrupt. The debt can be staggering.

Renunciation is the diversion of these funds, our life-energy, and transferring them to our spiritual bank account. Even at ten percent of our life-energy, the savings account can grow substantially. Ten percent of our time, ten percent of our energy, and ten percent of our interest is what traditional religion asks for, yet who is even ready to give that?

That would be two and a half hours a day, withdrawing the life-force from the body and senses and giving it to God. Most people would call such a person a fanatic! Yet this ten percent is the tithe that God asks for. This illustration is given to prompt us to think about how we spend our days, our time, and our life-energy. It is something to think about.

What most people do not realize is the tremendous payoff of this investment. The peace, happiness, and even higher productivity of worldly duties, come as a natural result of this investment.

As with most financial plans, the encouragement is to start today! Even if ten percent seems too high, start with five percent, or less, but start today! And be consistent, invest every day. What begins as a discipline and an act of will becomes a time of haven and necessity for our inner happiness and balance.

There is no one else to live our life for us! So, the decision must be, and always has been, ours. Let us determine to be a steady and consistent saver of life-energy for our spiritual bank account and watch our account grow. We will accrue unending peace, joy, and intuitive wisdom. Not a bad payoff in the here and now; not to mention the time when it comes to leave this body and world behind us. One day, with the balance of past debt paid, we will be free to come or go, but compulsory return will be a thing of the past. We will smile at that investment portfolio!

Loyalty

Loyalty is a timeless virtue, but it seems it is also timely. I have been asked in recent times what my view is on signing loyalty oaths. My view is that no realized spiritual master would require such a thing and it does not reflect teachings based on the highest Truth.

Loyalty is something that is earned, and if we want loyalty, then we must give it. But loyalty cannot be something that is mandated. The more one tries to demand loyalty, the more one reveals their deep-seated insecurity.

When we have a high level of respect and/or love for someone, loyalty is given naturally and freely. There are many instances in history of loyalty running so deep that one gives up their life for another. This must be said to be a very highly developed sense of loyalty when done for some noble purpose.

Today we tend to give little thought to loyalty. As long as things are working for us and we have some happiness, then we stay with a friendship, marriage, or work situation. But when things are not going quite the way we want them to, or when some other situation looks easier or better to us, then we leave our commitments and run to what promises to be expedient happiness.

This tendency to disloyalty when difficulties arise makes a deep impression on our soul. A pattern of such behavior will weaken our character and bring us suffering. Giving no loyalty to another, we see the world as unwilling or unable to give us loyalty. Deep down, we trust no one because we project our own inability to give loyalty onto others. Even if others show us loyalty, we will think them to be not very smart, to not have the courage to leave when they should, or always secretly scheming to get away or get revenge on us. It breeds a devious mindset that is always calculating the odds in our favor, or when we need to leave or find a scapegoat.

Loyalty, on the other hand, provides a solid core inside. When we go through difficulties with others, it tends to bring us closer together. As families experience crises and weather storms, they build a bond that they know can withstand practically any season; in business, in friendships, go right down the line and there are no exceptions to this rule.

Now that I have said that, I will say there is an exception, but it violates what loyalty is really built upon; that is when one stays loyal for the wrong reasons. What might those reasons be? Wrong reasons for staying loyal to others are when we are too fearful to separate; for reasons of greed, thinking we will get something by staying; for base reasons like lust or even revenge. But staying for these reasons is not loyalty; it is self-interest. Real loyalty cannot be compared to these pseudo-loyalties. Real loyalty will raise the soul up to a higher plane of consciousness that ennobles all whom it touches.

How can we compare such a lofty idea and ideal of loyalty to a demand that someone sign a piece of paper pledging their loyalty? I am surprised anyone can bring themselves to do it, even when they feel such loyalty to an individual or an organization. It flies in the face of the kind of relationship that creates a sense of trust, respect, and mutual regard that engenders loyalty. I can only believe that any who propagate such practices are not on good terms with loyalty and how it is generated. For myself, I would rather the world abandon me in time of need than for any to feel bound to me because they signed a piece of paper.

When my own Guru went through much physical suffering and many started to stay away, she never spoke ill of one person. Once in a while, she would say, "You know, I have been missing so and so." It was not that she had no feelings; she loved more deeply than anyone I have known. But it was an impersonal love that did not infringe on another's deciding power to come or go. She always held out the highest ideal for all and would do her best to help everyone live up to that ideal. She would teach, suggest, and speak very forcefully about her perception of truth, but she always left it up to the individual do to what they thought best. She gave all who came to her respect, love, and the loyalty of a truly realized teacher. In return, she expected the same. But when others did not live up to their best and did not reciprocate that loyalty as students/disciples, she let them go gracefully.

I cannot imagine that anyone would stay with something because they signed a piece of paper, and if they did stay for that reason, would they be the kind of person we would want to stay? All of these thoughts have come about as a result of listening to some others who encountered these rules from some different spiritual organizations. It is always timely to contemplate, meditate, and spend some time on the meaning of loyalty. What does it mean to be loyal? How do we know when to commit ourselves to being loyal? Are there times when loyalty is not really loyalty, but a form of cowardice or some other less-than-noble reason for staying with someone or something?

When I came to this path at twenty years of age, I had not given much thought to the idea of loyalty. Mother would mention it in her talks, and when I thought about it, my mind would always go to this sense of knowing when I was on the right track—following that inner direction. Mother would point out that loyalty to the inner guru always came first; this inner sense of knowing what was right was my inner guru. But that inner barometer of truth was not all that existed in me. I was also full of desire nature, fears, and uncertainties, undefined regions of thought and feeling. So, Mother also gave me guidelines designed to put me in touch with a more refined sensitivity to this inner knowing. It is like learning what is healthy for the body. When I am eating a lot of junk food, I will taste a carrot and not think it is very sweet. But when I clean my system of sugary items, that same carrot will taste very sweet. Staying "loyal" to a diet free of the sugary items will prepare the body to recognize the sweet taste of the carrot.

Spiritual disciplines and guidelines are like switching from a diet high in sugar to appreciating natural sweetness. When I was inundated with stimulation through the senses and by my desire nature, my sensitivity to my Spiritual Nature was blunted. By following the simple rules Mother proposed and focusing my mind in the way she guided me, my awareness of that inner guru grew. I did not know the Truth of all that Mother taught from the beginning. By staying loyal to her teachings, I garnered the experiences that showed me that what she taught was, and is, the Truth. Loyalty to her teachings changed my nature and refined my perception of Truth. I found the Truth discovered within and what was taught to me by Mother to be one and the same.

The movement or flow of energy in a group of people goes through ups and downs. All things in the world change: the weather, what is being talked about, enthusiasm, everything. When we join a spiritual group, there may be a lot of fresh energy flowing that sweeps many people up in its grip. When the predictable ebb of energy comes into the picture and the energy is more difficult to feel, either individually or collectively, then those who were there for the "ride" of the energy current will drop off. When we go through an individual or group crisis of down energy, loyalty and commitment are put to the test. These are the times that build that solid base of character, or we enter the quicksand-shifting loyalty of convenience.

The reason that loyalty is so critical to the sadhaka is due to the fact that no real spiritual progress can occur without the kind of commitment that comes with loyalty. I overheard a participant at a retreat talking about his spiritual path. This individual was in charge of some kind of a "spiritual" center. He said, "I can't really meditate. I am into Krishna Das (the singer) right now." Now, what kind of aspirant is that, and how far do you think he will go in his spiritual journey? With that kind of loyalty, he will be on to the next thing that captures his attention, and he has set himself up to lead others on their spiritual path—quite amazing.

Mother described a period she went through: for three years, she questioned her Master's spiritual attainment. She was a Center Leader and was holding meditations in her home. During that time, she mentioned her doubts to no one. She continued on with her spiritual practices and served all who came to her. Through her steadfast approach, she came out of that doubt and realized the incredible influence Master had on her life and what she had inwardly attained. She saw that attainment would not have been possible if not for Master and what he had given her. Her loyalty to her Guru and her steadfastness to her inner Guru of Truth weathered the storm and brought her to a greater degree of realization. It was not a blind faith that took her through the crises, but a sincere search for Truth combined with loyalty to the inner and outer guru.

All sadhakas will have crises of faith. These wilderness times will be some of the most difficult experiences we will have to face. It is loyalty that will see us through those times. Not a blind loyalty, not a faltering loyalty, but a loyalty first to Truth, and therefore to our spiritual path. When each experience we encounter drives us deeper into our search for Truth, then we will find what we seek. If we are "loyal" for the wrong reasons or that loyalty is misplaced, it will be shown to us in our search for Truth. For example, Sri Yukteswar asked young Yogananda to bring him back to the path if he found that he, Sri Yukteswar, was faltering on the path. What humility the great Master had. But also, he was teaching Yogananda about the complete loyalty of friendship, for that is what one friend does for another. When we have such loyalty for one another, no one will be a stranger; we will see our Beloved within all. Loyalty of this kind cannot be demanded, but only freely given. Indeed, it is the most precious gift in the world.

The Universal Religion

My great Guru Mother Hamilton often said, "There is one God, one religion." It has also been said that one person's myth is another person's religion. Myth in this case implies a fable, something not true, and religion means it is true. Thus begins the never-ending argument over religion. These discussions follow one of two veins. One: "My religion is truth, and your religion is false." Or: "Your religion has some truth, but mine is the truer, and to be truly spiritual or saved you should follow mine." With this religious superiority, the world is divided into camps; sometimes spilling over into war or protracted separation.

We have to ask ourselves, "Is this what God truly wants for his children of the earth?" I propose it is not, and further, I propose there is a way out, without anyone having to give up their religion—their pathway back to God.

That every great religion is humanity's approach to the Divine Nature as the real source of origin is intuitively understood. Each religion and subdivision of those religions vary in philosophy, language, and ritual to either a small degree or in large measure. These differences are compounded by a provincialism that says, "My way is the right way or the only way." And: "When I see the variances in language, philosophy, and customs, I am even more convinced you are wrong, and I am right."

In order to understand there is but one God and one religion, we must be able to identify what is common to all religions. Through identifying universal principles, universal truths, we can then speak of a universal philosophy that varies by language and customs only. It may be said that the color of skin may vary, but all humans bleed red. If God be truly the Creator of all, then equally there will be universal aspects to the heart and soul of humanity.

> **Postulate One:** There is a right way and a wrong way, or a superior way and an inferior way, of understanding the nature of creation and our individual relationship to it.

> **Postulate Two:** Religion addresses itself to those in error, or with inferior understanding, with an eye to teaching individuals the right way to approach their life.

> **Postulate Three:** By following these teachings, a change will be effected that will lead to the rectification of the previous fallen state into a condition of being saved and/or transformed.

> **Postulate Four:** The spiritual health of individuals and the community depends on the acceptance and implementation of the teachings.

These four postulates, I would submit, are universal to all the major religions. The common point that applies to all religions may be said to be the establishment of the spiritual health of the individual and the community at large.

There is an obvious point to be made here. All individuals hold beliefs, by and large, because they truly think those beliefs represent the highest truth. If they did not believe that they would change their beliefs. The two exceptions to this rule are due to individuals either being too lazy to think things through, or too fearful to change due to social pressure.

First Principle of Universal Perspective

The number one principle of a universal perspective should be the recognition that all individuals have a right to their beliefs. It should be assumed that each individual's belief represents their sincere effort at creating their own spiritual health as well as that of the community. There are, of course, those who are indifferent, or in antipathy, to the direct spiritual health of themselves or the community. Yet those too should be thought of as doing their best at creating some good for themselves and/or others. Barring direct harm they incur on others, which secular law should address, they should be allowed to believe as they see fit.

Finding Points of Agreement

In the pursuit of universal understanding, we may ascertain areas of universal principles that comprise a healthy spiritual life and community.

The three areas of Universal Spiritual Life are:

1. **Worship**

   All religions seek to direct the mind to some transcendent Being or Consciousness. Whether it be called God, Allah, Satchidananda, The Tao, Nirvana, or any number of designations, this worship or meditation upon this transcendent principle is core to any religion. Typically, there are centers of worship: a church, synagogue, temple, mosque, etc. For these places of worship to be respected and remain invariably protected, by one and all should be the watchword of all religions. In return, the keepers of these holy places should protect the sacred purposes for which they are created and not violate that sacred trust by becoming involved as centers for secular foundations, such as revolutions.

2. Love and Compassion

Not only do the great religions speak to the worship of a transcendent principle, but they also relate these principles to humankind: one's brother and sister. All too often, these universal sympathies become constrained by local identification. "Only those of my belief or community or country are deserving of my love and compassion." All great religions and religious leaders call on us to expand our love and compassion to one and all. Are we not called upon to emulate the great ones in whose steps we follow and find the means to love all? Surely universal love and compassion must be the foundation for a universal outlook.

3. Learning From Our Differences

The variety of ways of striving for the higher ideal can and does add richness and interest to all who strive to follow a high road. When an individual is truly secure in his or her own way, that individual can then afford to examine the ways of another. Our attempts to "live the one life" meet with challenges and obstacles on every front. Who is to say he or she has the best answer to every dilemma?

To learn and derive inspiration from those sincere in their desire to follow their spiritual way is wise and efficient. Sorting through externals and perceiving the essential principles, in addition to following one's own way, one may then find applying the ways of another an added means toward accomplishing the difficult task.

We can marvel at the wonderful and diverse ways individuals have evolved to worship the one God of all. Of course, not all ways will appeal to us equally and some we may find repulsive. But we can go back to the number one principle of a Universal perspective: respect for everyone's right to worship as they feel inwardly directed.

In supporting Universal ways of practicing beliefs and allowing for the practices of others in their religion, a very important phenomenon will happen. By uniting the efforts of those interested in the spiritual health of a community, that community's spiritual health will grow. Kindred spirits who differ on some philosophies but have agreement on some core principles will strengthen the community in living those principles.

Jointly aspiring for higher-mindedness, universal sympathy, and purity of lifestyle will advance the health and well-being of all. Acknowledging the areas of agreement will strengthen those areas for all. Leading a religious life, showing tolerance for differences but strength in principles, will inspire others to do the same. A knitting together of those who are pursuing the spiritual health of a community can only mean good for the community.

As our world shrinks with improved travel and communication, the imperative for not only tolerance of others but for the reinforcement of universal spiritual principles, becomes essential to the spiritual health of all. Spiritual health is under terrific attack today. There is one banner under which that attack may be defeated, and spiritual health established: one God, one religion. This is not to say all religions become one religion. It does mean a recognition of the one religion of humanity: the individual's relationship with his or her Creator.

There are many roads leading to a City of Light upon the hill. Let travelers by diverse roads lend support and inspiration to one another so that all may reach that blessed destination.

You Are a Divine Instrument

We are told the two-fold path to realization comes through dispassion for things of the world while keeping attention fully focused on God. The end result is a perfect union between the self of individuality and the Self of Universal Consciousness. This union brings about a condition in which the stillness of absolute Spirit and the activity of creation is seen as a singular existence of one absolute reality, God. With this vision, the whole of humanity, creation, and formless Spirit are all seen as seamless Divinity.

What is required for this Universal Vision is the two-fold purification of the mind from all limiting attachments. Thus, the two-fold approach of dispassion for things of the world, and a complete focus on God. In the lives of many realized Beings, an itinerate lifestyle was adopted, with the simplest of needs for the body begged from others in order to free the mind from worldly concerns so as to keep the focus on God. This life cannot and should not be adopted by all. Lahiri Mahasaya came as an example of one who lived in the world as a Householder, yet remained "Not of the world," keeping his spiritual freedom in the midst of activity.

The problem encountered by sadhakas aspiring for the Universal Vision is to make their way in the world yet remain out of the snare of attachment. Marriage, home, children, business, and social life tend to draw the mind outward, enmeshing it in attachment to things of the world. How does one then enter into the field of activity and remain free?

The answer to this question is the substance of the Householder's sadhana. The method described as the outer renunciate rejecting the world and its lures will not be effective for the Householder. The Householder moves right into the world's activities. The means of viewing this activity, voluntarily chosen, will differ for the Householder. All aspirations for the world may be seen by the Householder as willed by the Divine.

For Householders, acceptance of Divine Will through the desire nature is not license for an "anything" attitude. Rather, it requires a keen sensitivity to separation between the observer of a desire and the desire itself. Through inward acknowledgment that this desire comes from God, we as the Householders should feel an inner connection to the Divine and a loosening of identification with the ego nature. This inward freedom of Spirit is the keynote from which the Householder may gauge the effectiveness of this practice.

We can then feel more an instrument of Divine Will. In the beginning, start with the big picture of life. Are our goals sought in alignment with good and positive qualities? Whether it be marriage, raising of children, career, or social activities, are they of a high spiritual quality? To say we are leading an inwardly spiritual life but spending time and effort on a useless or destructive lifestyle is hypocrisy. To say we aspire for God-realization but are contemplating marriage to an abuser of drugs or someone engaged in other negative behavior just does not make sense. Bringing life goals into alignment with spiritual values begins the inner/outer congruity of Divine Will.

Next comes adherence to a spiritual method or discipline. We all know that to make progress in a chosen field, we must dedicate time and effort toward that goal. The greater we are consumed by a goal, the more likely we are to make progress. There are those who have prenatal talent that makes the accomplishment of a goal very easy for them in that field. This is both a blessing and a caution. Sometimes, the prize of spirituality does not go to the hare who makes rapid progress with just a little effort, but to the plodding turtle who takes one step after another, never giving up! Make meditation a humble surrender to the vast field of spirit that seeks to make its Sacred Goal known to the devotee.

With the goals of life correctly calibrated for a spiritual life and the daily practice of meditation and prayer in place, then we may reasonably look to the movement of Spirit throughout the day. In those times of meditation when we feel a great sense of peace and attunement—versus those times when it seems like wild horses have taken us for a ride and then ran us over—a natural kind of knowing will be present. Reflecting on certain situations, conversations, or choices in life—feel the rightness or wrongness of it all. It may come as a "gut feeling;" we just *know*. Most often, the thought of a situation will spontaneously come to mind, and we know what is in the highest alignment.

This intuitive knowing comes more often as we listen and respond to it. Living according to this inner direction brings a sense of alignment from ourselves to our Self. A certain feeling of purity emanates from the inside out, along with peace. These manifest qualities affirm that we are on the right track. Others may comment that they feel peaceful when around us, or they can always count on our opinion; it just seems to be always in the right direction.

This is the place for another caution. We can start feeling quite full of ourselves at this point. The sense of peace, purity, and wisdom can trigger the ego into thinking, "I've made it. I've arrived at that stage of perfection." It can be an overt thought or one that is lurking in the shadows, giving a certain smugness or secret arrogance.

The safest route here, as always, is a humble recognition that: "I of myself am nothing; it is my Father who doeth the works." The guru role can be an enormous help here. By surrender to the guru as teacher and guide, the right attitude is brought to the fore. No matter what your degree of spiritual development, the guru is acknowledged as the reason for that progress—easily give all credit to him or her.

This inner surrender helps inoculate us from spiritual pride. This does not create any sense of inadequacy or low self-esteem. Because the humble recognition is based on truth, it is a simple acknowledgment of a fact. Spiritual masters and God have no need or desire for groveling and pandering. True humble recognition that the power and feeling of God have come and remain with us as a result of a deep inner surrender is essential to growth. This attitude, applied to the movement of God through us, will bring happy harmony with Divine Law and Spirit.

By deepening attunement with the Divine Presence within, we will feel its guidance throughout the day. Easy compliance and alert recognition of this guidance strengthen its role in life to the point to where we feel but a witness to the Spirit within. Those times we fail to recognize intuitive direction from the Superconscious mind, or deliberately go against it, produce such painful circumstances that we grow more determined, stating that, "no matter what," we will adhere to God's will; even if that means the death of this body—death is preferred to the painful absence of the Divine Presence. This wholehearted commitment makes us a perfect instrument of Divine Will.

Feel that we are the machine and God is the operator. Far from making us a mind-numb automaton—feel more alive, more conscious, and more at peace. Be a witness to the fascinating drama of life as it unfolds within and without. In perfect surrender, let us feel as if we are a musical instrument played by a master musician. Become boundless in our experience and feel more and more that, "I am nothing; God is everything."

However, this does not lead to extinction; rather, we identify with the nature of God. What God is, so are we—Infinite, eternal, all-powerful, and all wisdom. The drop enters the sea; it ceases to be a drop but knows itself to be one with the sea. The sea also contains the drop, so may express itself as the drop if it wishes or may explore vast realms of itself.

For example, if we are learning a new task, say playing the piano, we may focus our full attention on our right hand in working to master the finger movements of a certain piece of music. In a high state of concentration, we may lose all conscious awareness of the room and the whole rest of our body except the fingers on our right hand. Over and over, we go through the movement of the right hand to be able to play those notes correctly. In that moment of concentration, we could say the whole world has become our right hand. As far as our conscious awareness is concerned, this is true, although the rest of our body continues all of its normal functions as always. When we release the concentrated attention from our right hand, our awareness returns to whole-body consciousness. At that time, we become aware that our right leg went to sleep because of the way we were sitting, it's a little bit warm in the room, etc. All things we were unaware of when focused so intently on our right hand.

Even so has the Divine All-consciousness become focused on our form and thought patterns, etc., to the exclusion of the universal omniscience. The All-conscious Being makes Himself unconscious as inert gases. Then He gradually becomes more and more conscious through minerals, vegetables, animals, and then humans. Like the practicing pianist awakens his or her hand to be an instrument of intelligent life-force until it can deftly play beautiful notes, so does the awakening God practice through His human instrument, making it a capable conduit of more and more refined consciousness. Gradually, the human body is fitted to express the highest consciousness even as God is! No longer the walking dead, the son of man, the human ego, has transcended into the Son of God, the Divine Manifestation—this is the fulfillment of the awakened one, the Buddha, the Christed one.

We are now fit to be the Divine Instrument for the ages. Divinity has at last found full expression through its human instrument. The steps toward this attainment as outlined earlier are available to all. The question is, "Who is willing to make the effort to become that fully awakened instrument of Divinity?" The calling is here today, as it ever has been. Who will hear? "Awake, Arise!"

Moral Courage

The development of moral courage is the essential basis for a spiritual life, without which all advanced practices are doomed to crumble and fall. The moral tenants have been known to us since time immemorial in various forms such as the Ten Commandments of the Bible and the Yamas and Niyamas of Patanjali.

Laws upon laws are piled upon the people of a nation by humans, but simple observance of basic morality with a courageous, selfless attitude would replace the millions of words of complex and conflicting law. To tell the truth, even when it goes against one's interest, is a basic for the spiritual aspirant. This does not mean we need to blurt out whatever comes to mind in the name of truth, no matter who it hurts, for this goes against another law: non-injury to others. This is most beautifully summed up as the Golden Rule: "Do unto others as you would have them do unto you." In fact, if this one Golden Rule were to be universally observed, it would single-handedly replace all other laws. Just think of a world where other people's interests were important to all! How this world would change.

"But," says the pragmatist, "that is not how the rest of the world is. If I were to take that attitude, I will be crushed by the greedy and careless!"

What do the spiritual masters advise us on this count? Jesus said the greatest thing a man can do is lay down his life for his fellow man. (John 15:13) In what way did Jesus lay down his life? He did it through total surrender to the Divine Will. He bore the slander and defamation from others in silent love. He may have lost the battle of the moment, but he won the war by shaping the world through his example.

But, he was not reticent to speak and act against misdeeds when he felt prompted; he was no coward. Indeed, he reflects the teaching of another world teacher, Krishna. Krishna says we must enter the arena of conflict when called as a duty. (Gita 1:31) To avoid conflict from ignorance that leads to reticence does harm to ourselves and the world at large. Jesus drove the money changers from the temple because they destroyed the holy vibration of a sacred temple. Thus, we must stand up for what is right, even give our life for that purpose if called upon.

We live with the courage of our conviction and surrender to Divine Will. This courageous morality comes to us through practice, just like using muscles in exercise strengthens the muscles through use.

Which of us has not succumbed to the temptation to lie when caught with guilt, shame, or an unwillingness to face the consequences of our actions? Each time we give in to moral weakness, we deflate our moral muscle. Conversely, each time we step onto the field of action and plainly speak the truth with injury to none, then we strengthen that muscle. Each time we treat another with the same care and consideration we would like to have shown to ourselves, we glow a little brighter. The moral muscle is gradually transformed from the muscular noodle of a weakling to the courage of a warrior's strength!

As spiritual aspirants, we must give due consideration to developing and perfecting our moral courage. The first step is to stop all dishonest behavior, make amends where we can, and leave the rest behind. Then we set our lives in order so that any action of ours may be shouted from the rooftops and not cause us shame or regret.

Next, practice every day with every person to treat them as we would like to be treated. As Jesus says, it is easy to love those who love us, what is tough is to love those who hate us. (Luke 6:31–35) This is a great test of our moral strength. We can be wise as a serpent—that is, we can avoid those who mean us harm, or we can hiss if necessary, rattle our tail in warning—but we are harmless as the dove. (Matthew 10:16) We don't return hate for hate, but prayerful love for hate. When we exercise our moral courage in this way, we glow with righteousness. This is the way to grow in God.

After all, how long has the Infinite put up with our insolence, indifference, neglect, and abuse? How would we have known to be different if not by the example of those spiritual souls that have gone before us? It is said that the Buddha had five hundred lifetimes of compassionate service to others before his shining example as the Buddha, the Anointed One! Are we to not follow in those hallowed footsteps? Surely, we are called. Who will follow?

Moral courage does not come naturally; selfish action to protect self-interest and the body is what is natural. The child gains in self-awareness and learns to say: "Mine!" This attachment continues as the natural way to be, into adulthood. It is not the natural way of worldly attachment we are called to live by, but the spiritual way of Divine giving. With developed moral courage, we overcome lower tendencies and become free and joyful spirits obeying a higher principle. May that moral courage so grow in us that it becomes a glowing example for all to follow and we can one day replace inferior human laws with a few simple verities of the Absolute.

Compassion

Compassion is the very watchword of saints and realized masters. Compassion is the extension of empathy for all suffering. In gaining realization of our oneness with the all-pervading Reality, it is realized that there is no difference between ourselves and all that we survey. Realized Beings have experienced existing as blades of grass over which people walk, they feel the vibration of stone and mountain while knowing it is not inert matter but living substance with vibration, consciousness, and spirit! With this expanded sense of identity, how could the Realized Beings not have an identification, understanding, and compassion for all suffering? It would be literally impossible.

There are those who, once gaining their realization, make a vow to continue to come back to this sphere where ignorance reigns in order to help those suffering from that ignorance to gain realization as well. Such is the love and compassion produced in such ones. In that pursuit of awakening humanity, fully realized Beings take on a garb of flesh and ignorance for the sake of humanity. They will see themselves, at least for a time, as separate from the realized state they hold so dear. With a crushing sense of confinement, they voluntarily focus their attention on a tiny mass of flesh and bone and identify with that, leaving behind their omnipresence, their bliss, their absolute oneness with the whole. The narrow confines of this state of ignorance, so newly worn, chafes against their freedom-loving nature. They feel themselves driven to regain the lost status of their Divine Heritage. Similar in nature to those souls who are nearing their "final mile" of realization, these great Beings enact the drama of gaining their realization once again. Oftentimes, they take on a much greater load of karma than the average individual, for they have come to pay the price of ransom for many. Far from having an easier time of it, since their cloak of ignorance has been so newly donned, they suffer greater extremes. Like the adults who take a load from their children's backpacks when they tire on a hike—so does the Realized master assume the burden of those who God has brought to them for help on their way.

More than others, these compassionate masters realize the paradise lost by all humanity. They know the huge loss entailed in suffering through narrow identification of body consciousness. They yearn to awaken us all to our real nature. But they find that although suffering abounds, most want to continue sleeping. Rather than the suffering spurring on the desire to awaken, the sleepyheads only roll over for some more sleep, asking for a happier dream! So, humanity dreams on. What can be done? Free will is the birthright of each soul. Our Mother Hamilton was such a one, a soul who came of her own free will. Not compelled by the law of cause and effect, only the law of compassion brought her to this vale of tears.

She, along with her great Guru, Paramhansa Yogananda, came to awaken humanity from their terrible sleep.

In the same century that was graced with great spiritual masters and scientific advancements, it was also a century stricken with unparalleled suffering. It is said that Adolph Hitler killed twenty million people, Lenin twenty million, Joseph Stalin forty million, and Mao Tze Tung topped them all with sixty million. The additional horror to all? Most of these deaths were not of victims of war with another country, but of those who lived within the borders of the very same countries as these vicious leaders. It is an unaccountable mystery, how a Hitler, Lenin, Stalin, and Mao can coexist on the same planet as a Mahatma Gandhi, Paramhansa Yogananda, Mother Hamilton, and Babaji.

I believe that it was not only brave individuals giving their lives for freedom on the battlefield that has seen the brutality of these movements beaten back again and again, but the sacrifice of these great spiritual masters as well. These spiritual masters came at a crucial time in history. With the rapid development of scientific intelligence, in combination with these dark forces unleashed on the earth, the world could have easily seen ruthless dictators with nuclear weapons. And could there be any doubt that if any one of these cruel and ruthless leaders were in sole possession of such weapons, they would have hesitated to use them to advance their own selfish interests and self-aggrandizement? It is a dark thought to think of Hitler in sole possession of nuclear bombs and rockets. Master once stated that it was Jesus and Babaji who planted the idea in Hitler's vain mind to attack Russia. Without that blunder, it is very conceivable that Hitler would have overwhelmed Britain and had the time to develop not only the intercontinental missile, but nuclear weapons as well.[19] What a different world this would be!

---

19   That, along with Germany's declaration of war on the United States rank as two of the greatest blunders made by Hitler. Master said they also tried to stop the war, but karmic forces and human free will swept nations into the onslaught.

True spiritual masters are ever helping the world to come into its rightful inheritance of the Kingdom of Heaven. But equally so, the supreme Creator has endowed each soul with free will. It is soul choice, individually and collectively, what kind of world we create. Really, we have everything needed to make this a paradise on earth. But the human heart must change from selfish self-interest to universal compassion. Think of the resources wasted in wars and conflict, and the intelligence and creativity employed for destructive ends. If this human genius can be focused on health, physical, mental, and spiritual, we could indeed have a heaven on earth. Simple laws of behavior make it so. Jesus summed it all up with the teaching to love God above all else, and to demonstrate that love toward all of humankind. If we emulated even a portion of the compassion that these great masters show us, how we, and this world, would change. We could not lie to another, cheat, steal, commit adultery, or even hurt and destroy our bodies through drugs, alcohol, or other destructive habits.

Compassion is not being a mush-head. It does not mean that feelings rule our actions. Rather, it is the clear knowledge that we cannot separate our own interests from all those around us. There is a saying that you "do not foul your own nest." Well, this world is our nest: not just our little family unit, but the world is our family; not just our local community, but the world is our community. In these days of overstimulation by the media, that may seem too much. But that is because we try to grasp the idea with our mind. Rather, it is something to be grasped by the spirit. We can start by opening ourselves to those around us. We can do this silently, inwardly, by simply making forays of conscious compassion to the world around us. Most of us exist with a covering around us, around our hearts. We have toughened ourselves as proof against being overwhelmed by the misery within us and in the world at large. What will protect us in the forays of compassion? It is by first becoming established in Spiritual Consciousness.

Now that does not need to be an overwhelming assignment in itself! It can be quite simple. Let us start by feeling oneness with the heart of God, very simply, right inside our own heart. See the world as God must see this world. Most people wear veneers of knowing what they are about, but inside, they are not at all certain. We can feel ourselves in touch with a capacity for empathy for this human condition while, of course, including ourselves in this compassion as well. Remaining above it all, yet intimately connected with the pain and suffering of all, feel the pulse of humanity. So that we do not drown in the emotions of it all, it is important that we keep ourselves separate from it as well as connected with it. With conscious awareness, we feel the rhythms of all humanity, but even more so we feel Divine Compassion. From that compassion flows a continual stream of love. As the parent watches the child struggling to build something, the child wants no help, the wise parent realizes that the child must struggle on his or her own, and yet the parent can feel for the struggle of the child. There may be moments when a word from the adult here and there clears the way for the child, but timing is important. Likewise, struggling humanity is often not in need of advice, but wise compassion.

I have heard of a principle in physics that states: anything observed will be changed. Not through the intention of the observer, but as a natural course of nature. Human beings certainly fall under that principle as well. Whenever anything is observed, the observed will change. If the observer tries to change that which is observed, the observed oftentimes reacts with oppositional will. We can think of times when we have been on the receiving end of well-intentioned advice. Sometimes, even when we know it is sound advice, we may fight against it just out of general principle, being that the idea did not originate with us! But let someone be with us, compassionately, understandingly, and we will know the right thing to do spontaneously. Through acceptance from another, we learn acceptance of ourselves. Through self-acceptance, we automatically come into deeper touch with what our wisdom would naturally want us to know. From being compassionately observed, we find that we change automatically.

The purer the consciousness that is observing us, the more perfect a reflection we may see in our own soul. The more perfect the consciousness under observation, the more perfect a soul reflection may be seen by the observed. This is the principle underlying darshan. Darshan means literally "the sight of" another person. In India, it is being in the Presence of a realized Being. When a sincere devotee comes into the province of a realized Being, a transmission of compassionate Grace is transmitted to devotees, allowing them to know the true reflection of their Soul. The more refined the devotees, the more they may see for themselves their true Spiritual Nature. This is the Grace of being in the purified company of saints and realized Beings. To one who has no such sensitivities, they see an ordinary person and/or a reflection of themselves. However, the compassionate Grace flows to all alike.

Where East and West Meet

Why take on the ways of Eastern Mysticism when, born here in the West, we have traditions of the Judeo-Christians, Greek philosophers, and modern science philosophy? In my view, it is in the East, and particularly in India, that the true spirit of religion has been preserved. Not necessarily in the masses who attend religious fairs and practice temple worship, although, like all religions, men and women of Realization may be found in the outer reaches, here and there. Realized souls have kept ablaze the real purpose of life—conscious realization of God—and the means of achieving that lofty goal.

There is much evidence this was also part of early Judaism and Christianity. Mother Hamilton found a description of the Kriya Breath in the Old Testament. Jesus proclaimed the Kingdom of

Heaven is within, and in the Gospel of St. Thomas, he taught that, "The kingdom of heaven is spread all over the earth." Through Jesus saying, "Keep thine eye single and thy whole body shall be filled with Light," he was drawing the attention inward. But material humans, weighted with body consciousness, brought these inner teachings to a worldly status. True, if enough of humankind were to achieve Heavenly Consciousness, the world as a whole would become Heavenly. But Jesus said there would be some standing here that shall not pass away before the coming of the Kingdom. (Matthew 16:28) He did not preach, nor do I think the prophets proclaimed, a distant event. They were speaking of imminent reality. The Kingdom of Heaven is at hand! That truth *is*; it always has been. But countless millions look to a distant day, now Jews and Christians together, for over two thousand years. Even for God, this represents a bit of time. Does he have no mercy in his timing, so fraught with shattered lives?

I say no! His promise has been fulfilled and continues to be fulfilled. Saints of all times and places have experienced the second coming and continue to do so. These are not dead promises, nor are they speaking of some unfulfilled future. They are living words demanding action and vigilance today. But what action? Certainly, we know the Ten Commandments, or at least we should, and we know the Golden Rule, (whether we practice it is a different question). We may say Grace before eating and when we attend church on Sunday. Beyond that, what do we do?

That is the question answered in the science of Yoga. It teaches that the Kingdom of Heaven is within, a state of Being to be realized, and it teaches the means for realizing it. For although it may be rightly said the Kingdom comes as a gift of Grace, nevertheless it requires the utmost effort to attain it. Are these not contradictory statements of fact? (No, in fact, they are both true.) Humans cannot, through their own effort, create or make the Kingdom of Heaven manifest. The fact is: it is our inheritance; it is built into us from our first inception as an individual soul. No amount of effort can take away from it nor add to it. It is ours already, a fact of Grace by design.

But, we must come of age to be able to accept our inheritance. It is like a young boy who is given the finest sports car in the world as a gift from his father. The boy in fact and in theory has the car, but really it cannot fulfill its real meaning and purpose for the boy until he has grown to maturity, both physically and emotionally. He first gets a tricycle, then a bicycle with training wheels, and so on; he progresses to more sophisticated modes of transportation. It would be a foolish and negligent father who gave the boy access to the most powerful and sophisticated car in the world on his sixteenth birthday. No, the father is going to look for signs of maturity, skill, and balance as the boy continues to work his way up to his inheritance.

So must we, as souls, work our way up in consciousness, proving as Jesus' story of the talents, we use what we have well. Otherwise, we may cause ourselves and others greater harm by having more than we have proven we can handle. When we are ready, we are given more. If we squander what we have been given, then even that which we have been given will be taken away. Harken well to this lesson; the law is exacting. But if we use well what we have been given, we receive more to work with. For Kriyabans, this means to exercise to full effect what we have been given. And, when experiences come and we handle them well by cultivating humility, selfless service, love, and wise decisions, and we fulfill our duties to the world and to God, then we earn greater capacity in God.

The wisdom of the East brings to us a guiding Light. We find the same seeds were cast into Judaism and Christianity, finding occasional flowering, but not the fullness realized in India. Why then, the material mind may ask, is India materially poor, and America materially rich? Like all nations, India has a karmic pattern. I doubt Jews or Christians of early eras would argue Rome's superior military and economic power proved it a superior spiritual power. But through all the dark times it has been subjected to, India survives with its universal outlook, realized Beings, and scriptural truths intact, dating back many thousands of years before our common era.

Yogis, those involved in worldly life and those separating themselves, even as Jesus did, from material possessions and relations, continue to hold aloft a Light for struggling humanity. And of all humanity, one here and there raises their head above the toil of the day to look to a further Light. And the Light, our inheritance, is there, waiting for maturing souls to come into their own. The East of India has kept both the goal and the means to the goal: i.e., methods of meditation, life-force control, pure love and devotion, sacred chanting, etc., in the forefront of their culture and philosophy.

The more I know of the sacred techniques and lore of India, the more I appreciate the wisdom of what I grew up with. Far from distancing me from Christianity, Judaism, Greek philosophy, or scientific philosophy, it has brought me closer to the beauty of what these have to offer. I find in what is called the Old Testament, beautiful truths of the highest nature. And the life and teachings of Jesus, the anointed of God, are filled with all the wisdom and perfection I find in the Eastern masters. In fact, the unfolding consciousness of humankind may draw inspiration from any of these wells, and others besides, and find themselves fed with the same sweet-tasting living waters of truth. To say the water from only one well will quench our thirst, or that other wells are filled by human effort and only our well by God's Grace, would be arrogant and shortsighted.

Would an omniscient God not provide the means of salvation, realization of our oneness with Him, to all people at all times when a sincere desire was present to do so? Who could look at the various religions of the world and say God forsook all but a chosen few? This would hardly prove to be just, or even make sense to a little human perspective, much less to a Divine one. Through God's Grace, we have available wisdom of the East that is also latent in all we have in the West. It is latent but not explicit. It is time for a grand awakening for all—everywhere. The need is great to establish the goal for humankind to fulfill their evolutionary destiny of

Realization to their highest Nature, to become fully engaged in self-less service, and to acknowledge the transcendent love of God—and through the love of God, love for all His creation. We may all partake of the method-means of the East while deepening our appreciation and understanding of the ways of the West. One supports the other. No vanity, jealousy, narrow-mindedness, or other obstruction need inhibit our focus on how God has provided for the salvation of all humankind, East, West, North, and South. May it be ever so! God, Christ, Gurus.

What is True Joy

What is the nature of true joy?
If all the nations call me blessed
This is not everlasting joy.
But if all nations should revile me,
Persecute me, sneer at me,
And I stand unaffected,
One with God,
That is true joy!

If friends and lovers
Should say sweet things,
Honor me with praise,
This is not enduring joy.
But if close intimates
Should betray me,
Seek to destroy me
And I am forgiving in my heart
That is true joy!

If I should have all wealth,
Success and fame come my way,
Associates seek my favor and advice,
All the world, as it were,
Sits at my feet
That is <u>not</u> unfading joy.
But if fame and fortune desert me,
And my love remains complete
That is true joy!

If health and pleasure
Heap their bounty upon me,
And I say, "life is good,"
This is not absolute joy.
But if sickness visits me,
Beauty fails me, old age overtakes me,
And residing in my Spirit I say, "Life is good!"
That is true joy!

If I were to lead a good life
And at the end of my days
I enter the Heavenly Abode,
This is not supreme joy.
But if I were to live a life of slavery
And at the end, God should put me in hell,
And I saw some good I might do there,
And I felt gratitude to God for the opportunity,
<u>That</u> is true joy!

Yogacharya David

PART TWO

Awaken the Light of the World

Be in silence. And from that silence, see the Light of the world, that Light which lighteth every man and woman, and can awaken Itself in the world. Let that Light shake off sleep's angel's dust and awaken to a mighty roar! See that Light shining in your hands, your feet, your whole body, mind, and the altar of your heart. Then see sparks of that fiery wave jump to others, and from them to others still, awakening in them their own sleeping Light. Like a conflagration, that Light spreads over the world, awakening joy, peace, right thoughts, and activity. The darkness of past ignorance seems as a dream. All the world arises to be a City of Light upon the hill. Every individual's antenna of heart and mind is attuned to that frequency of Light and harmony. "Arise, Awake!" is the thunderous call. "Forsake sleep and know your Divinity as never before."

Bring the power of God within you and know that this world is in for change. Be on the crest of that wave of change and ride it in joy! Hari Om Tat Sat

Every Day

Every Day I will work on perfecting myself in You.
Everyday Day I will take steps rightly guided toward Your domain.
Every Day I will surrender my efforts to Your Infinite Will.

Every Day I am Your child, who knows I am loved and cared for.
Every Day Your Light illumines me, and through me, the world is
illumined.
Every Day You live Your life through me.
And, Every Day, You and I are One, and blessedness reigns
supreme.

Two Thieves Steal Inward Sight

Two thieves steal from us inward sight
Closing our eyes to earthly pleasures and woes,
Yet focusing the attention on the One
We move inward the spinal Way.

Breathing slows
Mind stills
Heart rests
Hush, calm is here.

Lightning flashes in darkness,
Stream of Aum floods silence,
Constrained mind expands,
Blissful joy rises within.

Now inner revelation unfolds,
Unspeakable truth makes itself known,
Transformation makes me new
At last, I know my Self true.

Truth comes in such hidden Ways,
The world continues its preoccupations,
One here and there hears the call,
The world thus-wise becomes enlightened!

Scaling the Heights for Guru Darshan

Guru is the pure snow of white peaks above us. Guru shows Its grace by taking form as living waters in streams, rivulets, and mighty rivers. Some taste the waters, finding it good; they journey to the origin from where the waters run. Others try to dam up the river and say they are in charge of it, and all must come to them to drink. Such are religious institutions and factions. Others try to bottle the water and develop a brand name that others will buy. Such are the sectarian organizations and over-the-counter salesmen of God. Others say the water trickling through the dams and into the bottles is just ordinary tap water. Guru smiles at the play downstream, and weeps for those who are thirsty and denied water. So, rivers and streamlets, one after another, are formed to quench the thirst of all.

Dam builders and bottlers rush in profuse anxiety, decrying other sources or try to quickly contain them. But Guru really loves the intrepid who scale the heights, and enjoy the view from the peaks. Then, sometimes, one here and there says they will become a new stream for the guru. Guru is happy for He wants all to drink of the fresh living spring water, not the limpid dammed or bottled variety. And, perhaps another will so feel inspired by that taste to scale the heights for Guru's darshan.

Guru is not a person, place, or thing. Guru is Spirit. Guru is God. Guru is perfection. Human instruments of Guru grace this earth. They bring wisdom, teachings, and compassion to seekers every-where. Guru is universal. Guru cannot belong to anyone alone, although He feels as though there is only lover and beloved in all the world. That is because Guru is love itself.

Birds Herald a New Day

The chirps of birds herald a new day,
Streaks of dawn pierce the dark,
Heaviness of night yields
Blessed Day begins!

Inner awakenings stir deep,
Signs of change come gradual,
Yearning outdistances knowing
Dawn comes too slowly!

I stumble in pre-dawn hours,
But see my faults more clearly.
Hope alternates with despair,
Far too gradually does the sun come!

Sight now awakens
Stronger my steps grow,
I help one here and there
Those whose eyes are darkened still.

A new day dawns
The world awakens
And shakes off the dreamer's trance
Songs of praise resonate from high towers.

The sun is for all,
Fear abandons itself to gratitude,
Loneliness becomes omnipresence
And life knows joy anew!

What Presence Moves Within

What presence moves within?
Little do I know or realize
What wonders will come
In creeping Lightning streaks.

"Behold, I stand at the door and knock"
But who opens,
Who will open,
To inner Light and Beauty?

I, I open
Not to go out!
But to let Him in
I receive Him.

And in that communion
Of heart, of soul, of Spirit
A spiritual feast ensues,
Filled with love, wisdom, joy!

O what promise is there
To you and to me
But... who opens,
Who will open?

The feast is spread
And, who will receive
The universal One
Who knocks at our door?

Divine Love

Why do great spiritual masters emphasize Love as the path and goal of realization? Once having tasted Divine Love, all such discussion ends. The superior merits of Divine Love are not to be found in romance novels or even the glorious descriptions of poets. Music may be a stepping stone, but no expression of Divine Love can be Love itself. Blunted materialists and absorbed intellectuals alike are quickened when touched by this all-absorbing State of Being. Tiny candles and even powerful search lights are left useless when the sun arises, so do all expressions of humanity become dull and limpid compared to the charm of Divine Love. Jnanis leave their dry intellect; those in service stop in rapt awe; those worshipping images lose sight of the images; and all Raja Yogis lose their breath in silent communion. All of nature stops, absorbed in the All-absorbing Nature of Divine Love that is more than a feeling of emotion, more than a thought or relationship, more than words or ideas can express. Inexpressible, Divine, Pure, and rapturous It is.

The reason saints sing Its glories is due to It surpassing all other glories. It is truth to say that God and Love are One. Unless you have drunk deep of Its virtue, you cannot say you know It. But realized masters have, and continue, to drink deep of It. Yet, the more they drink, the more they have the capacity to drink deeper. It is endless. And they are calling. These masters are calling to you, me, all: "Come, drink with me!" In fact, I have drunk to the point that I, myself, I became that Love Itself. I look and see nothing but That. So, drink me if you will! For the more that is drunk, the more plentiful the supply. Let us all drink to satisfy and continue drinking so others may drink of us for we are That, and That is ourselves.

This is the calling of the Great Ones. Come, let us drink Divine Love!

O Lord, My Prayer

O Lord, Thou hast given me intelligence, reason, and feeling.
Please, O Lord, guide Thou my intelligence, reason, and feeling.
Thou hast also given power of will, movement, creativity, and energy.
Please O Lord, guide me in the use of will, movement, creativity, and energy.
O Lord, finally Thou hast given me things material: money, home, family and friends, and all possessions.

O Lord, make me a good steward of things material and a worthy member of the human race.
Thank You, Lord, for hearing my prayer, for I know You know my thoughts even before I do.
I pray this prayer to impress it into my own mind.
I pray not to change You; I pray to change my self!

Perfection Shining

The child's smile warms the hearts of all,
Reflects the smile of God;
The student who ardently learns something new,
Understands something of God's intelligence;
The mother who suckles a newborn babe
Gives the life of God through her love;
The father who protects and serves his family
Watches with the care of God;
The teacher who awakens new light in another
Does the work of God;
The mystic who becomes pure Spirit,

Shines God's Light for all;
When all humanity lives in harmony with
The all-pervasive One
Fulfilling their highest nature,
Then we shall see perfection shining all about.

Bhakti's Meditation

Meditation is really an inner absorption in the Divine. Many people are interested in meditation, but few attain that blessed state. All meditation has a common theme: that is, the sadhaka starts out with concentration. Usually, the point of concentration is on a mantra, a particular sound, or words. Higher teachings come through the place of attention when the attention is put on the anahata, heart center, or the ajna, the point between the eyebrows. The reason for this is: where the focus of the mind goes, there also flows the life-force of the body.

The flow of this life-force, prana, enlivens wherever it flows and increases awareness of that area. Both the anahata and ajna are focal points for spiritual awakening, along with the sahasrara, the crown of the head. By repeated attention to these areas, they begin to awaken. People usually focus on the five senses, sex, survival, and power of will: i.e., gaining name, fame, and wealth. These constitute the realm of ego. The first awakening of a transcendent nature is love. That love is usually focused on a sweetheart, children, or friends, but it can also be nature or perhaps a locality or a country. This love is usually a mixture of ego and some transcendent nature. Ego is based on self-interest: i.e., "If I love you, you will love me back." Transcendent love is, "I love you for your own sake and because it is my nature to love, not for what I get in return."

Divine love is the fullest expression of transcendent love. It is purified of ego considerations and the ledger book of quid and pro quo. Love becomes the very nature of the sadhaka, being a fulfillment unto itself. This is why the heart center is the first center in the upward ascension considered worthy of awakening spiritual growth.

The next center mentioned is the ajna, the point between the eyebrows. This area is universally acclaimed as the doorway to higher consciousness. It is here that one may enter into states of consciousness that transcend the sense of "I,"—that is, the idea of separation, and can then enter into the grand union of Spirit. "The light of the body is the eye: if therefore thine eye be single, thy whole body shall be full of light," said Jesus. (Matthew 6:22) In addition, "The light of the body is the eye: therefore, when thine eye is single, thy whole body also is full of light, but when thine eye is evil, thy body also is full of darkness." (Luke 11:34) This eye is the ajna, the astral eye of omniscience. This center is considered to be the most important center of transcendence and leads automatically to the sahasrara when entered.

The mantra used should be under the guidance of a guru. The guru has the consciousness to awaken the sadhaka's higher centers. Like inert metal that is exposed to a strong magnet, the inmost metal itself becomes magnetized, and so does the sadhaka become inwardly charged through the spiritual magnetism of the guru. This magnetism increases the positive draw to spiritual consciousness and helps to open these inner centers. In concert with the sadhana performed by the sadhaka, this inner draw works a secret alchemy that gradually purifies the mind of vasanas, desire nature, and latent downward tendencies. This sadhana is twofold. The first is to turn away from attachment to things of the world, vairagya, or inner renunciation. The second, to reorient the mind to higher consciousness, to make the mind inward or bhakti.

Meditation is one of the means to do this. By focusing on the ajna and refusing the pull to things of the senses, either in the body or in the imaginal body, we are practicing sadhana. But this practice is not easy to come by. Habit nature of body consciousness tends to be strong—after all, that is the place where we have lived most of our lives. And, the focus on the material world may have yielded some nice results. The other side of that is just pure fear of releasing the known world of the senses, even if it has mostly produced misery for us. These two lions, one desire nature, the other fear, stand at the door of inner consciousness. We may be mindful that these two lions are not a weakness of the sadhaka alone, but are universal to all seekers. Overcoming these opposing forces is the very stuff of which sadhana is composed.

As we know, there are four paths of Yoga: Yoga of action, Yoga of love, Yoga of discernment, and Yoga of life-force control. Each personality will naturally feel more drawn to Karma Yoga, Bhakti Yoga, Jnana Yoga, or Raja Yoga. And it may be that there will be a combination of all four. I like to think of our path as the Fourfold Path. That is, it uses elements from all four disciplines. And, even if your nature is oriented to Karma Yoga, selfless service, nevertheless, you can greatly benefit from Karma Yoga by Kriya Yoga meditation. Mother Theresa, a great Karma Yogini, spent early morning hours and evening hours in deep prayer and meditation. This time spent was essential to keep her focus truly on serving the Christ each day.

I was speaking to a social worker one day. She said rather off-handedly, "Oh yes, I used to do the Mother Theresa thing, then I burned out." Well, I doubted she really did the Mother Theresa "thing." Those hours Mother Theresa spent in God-communication with her focus on seeing the Christ in each one she met made her service very pure and was the source of seemingly boundless energy. That deep communion with God served as an inoculation against burnout. Whatever our main calling, we must cultivate that inner communion in order to keep balance, perspective, and clear focus. That communion comes through deepened prayer and meditation.

Learning to still the mind takes persistence and patience. We may make it a priority to first enter into prayer. When you go to visit a good friend, you start the visit with talking about important things in your life. You can cultivate friendship with God in the same way. You can talk over the day, important, trivial, and fun matters of your life. This cultivates an inner intimacy. If there are questions about your life, you may even spend time without talking. You may rest, do some hard work, or just sit quietly together. With God, too, you can spend time in silent contemplation. This moves us to a greater sense of intimacy. Do not feel that kind of intimacy should come "just like that." Most of us are not used to that much intimacy.

Imagine, if you will, cultivating intimacy with God as a gradual unfoldment, as the petals of a flower opening and surrendering themselves to the sun, rather than a picture of storming the castle gates to take possession of the city. It is not for God's sake that we go to this place, but our own. We can willingly surrender ourselves if we feel the absolute good inherent in what we are surrendering ourselves to. But if fear, guilt, and suspicion are in the mind, then surrender will seem like a battle. It does not need to be that way between us and that inmost Friendship. Here we can gently, calmly, go inwards in a way that suits us. Move around the edges, test the feeling nature here and there. Sit in the Presence at a little distance, then try moving a little closer. We may have innate fear and distrust; that is all right, just test the waters a little at a time.

When we are ready, and only when we are ready, we can ask God to come into us. We can open ourselves to exploring the ways this Spirit comes to us. Calmly observing, it may be different than we imagined. The differences can be noted. It may be enough intimacy for the moment, and we can enjoy exactly what it is. God is not going anywhere, He is right there, very willing to be with us exactly as we would like Him to be. Intimacy does not usually come in big, fantastic displays, but in gradual unfoldment. Learn to discern the subtle flavors of Spirit. Keep the focus right there. It is right under your breath, a sensation close to you, even a slight thrill throughout your body cells, a feeling of peace and gentleness. Cultivate this fine and delicious aroma. This is God come to you as a rare and gentle Spirit. This may be different than how you usually think of meditation. This is the heart and soul of a bhakti. God as friend, lover, intimate.

The Bhakti thinks of God's qualities, especially as an intimate. "O Lord, you are the Friend of all friends; you come with everything to give. You lack only one thing, that one thing I may give or withhold; that is my friendship, my love. O Lord, you are the beauteous feeling within, the glow of colors in nature. You are my all in all." In this way, Bhaktis talk to God. And as they say these things, the Bhaktis start to feel even more intimacy with the Beloved. A rapturous feeling can grow, an opening of the heart in a love song of Spirit that then subsides in a gentle manner into a caress. Rapt in this intimate world of lover and Beloved, that soul opens gradually to the love spreading out to all creation. The whole universe feels to be one's body, all throbbing in wonderous waves of joyful love. Free of body-limiting thoughts. Consciousness "centered everywhere, circumference nowhere." It knows Its Omniscient home once again. This universal embrace into omnipresent Love and Joy is the ultimate sacramental bond where lines of lover and beloved dissolve into the oneness of Love.

This rapture then descends again and lover and Beloved once again start their dance. Ever at one, ever apart do they dance and play, ever in the rapture of love. It is difficult to convey to one whose heart has not awakened to at least a hint of this dance. Perhaps a glimpse comes when one's heart and spirit are touched by some music, picture, or film. But earthly hearts are fickle: there today, gone tomorrow. God's heart is ever-ready; ours are unsteady, unrefined, inconstant. To make the attention steady, bringing all moods, thoughts, and awareness into that Divine Aura brings ultimate union. It makes no difference what the mood may be. One may be a lover, in anger, fearful, lonely; it makes no difference. The key is that one does not shrink from the Beloved through fear, shame, or, worst of all, indifference.

Only with a steady, meditative mind can that kind of devotion be brought to its fullness. This intense love affair is exemplified by Krishna, Christ, Ramakrishna, Saint Francis, Paramhansa Yogananda, and Mother Hamilton. In some, the love was transcendent only, never focused on a deity or image; such is the case with Krishna and Christ. In others, a deity or personality was the focal point, as with Saint Francis on Christ, and Mother Hamilton on Paramhansa Yogananda.

The devotee/lover of God with form must ultimately transcend that form. But the form plays a distinctive and important role in the devotee's life. That form becomes the focal point for the mind. A focal point like this is necessary for most. Even as children focus their attention on their mother most of all, so devotees find a focus for their object of love. This objectification needs to be understood in its right context. If it is seen as a doorway through which the devotee enters into universal consciousness, then it is rightly understood. If it leads to separation and sectarianism: such as, "My object of devotion is the only way, or the superior way, and your way, your religion, is inferior or wrong." Then it changes worship from sattvic, sweet devotion, to tamasic, or darkness. It can also lead to, "My religion is the only right way, and I am going to snub out all other ways." This is a rajasic tendency for domination. Neither the tamasic nor rajasic reflect true spirituality.

What is essential in any devotee is the true Spirit that comes with an open heart guided by wisdom. This may be recognized in a Christian, Hindu, Buddhist, Muslim, Jew, or in any of the countless theologies of the world. Within any religion, we may find those that are alive in an inner Spirit and Light. And Jesus said, "Not everyone that saith unto me, Lord, Lord, shall enter into the kingdom of heaven; but he that doeth the will of my Father which is in heaven." (Matthew 7:21) You may see such ones sitting here and there in congregations around the world. Their faces glow with Light; their hearts open, they are alive to an inner Light that cannot be denied and cannot be missed by one attuned to the Light. They reflect the qualities of Light: i.e., purity, softness of heart, standing by principle, inwardly directed. And, oftentimes, they are not the ones up in front, or on a board of directors. They may be, but they may just as easily be sitting in the back, or walking in the woods, or tending to someone who needs their care.

You see, this is the thing that defies circumscription by rule and law yet carries its own rule and law by its own virtue. Now ego can get a hold of that teaching and run rampant in a life of license. But devotees would not be doing the will of the Father in that case. To awaken inwardly to that Light, that Love, that devotion, is the meditation of the Bhakti. And, once fully awakened, it is a light unto itself. It guides, directs, accompanies, and comforts the devotee through thick and thin. Why? Because devotees have put God first, have meditated on love's ecstasy, and given themselves, heart, mind, and soul, to their Infinite Beloved. And it is a law: as ye give, so shall ye receive. When you give all, without expectation, you receive all unreservedly.

So, my blessed friends, learn the secrets of this open heart, be guided by the clarity of inner Light. Learn to meditate on love's ecstasy, and you will step into a world that is beyond the scope of human imagination. For it is a Divinely inspired world of Spirit that may be vouchsafed only to those who give their all. If you are lukewarm: "Oh I will meditate some; if I realize God sometime in the future, that's alright," then pray ardently that God makes you one of those awakened ones whose light will so shine, that it will be a beacon for all those thirsting to find the Light. Better to be clear: awaken to your Bhakti spirit even now, and know the inner glory of that Love and Bliss divine.

Just For Today

Just for today
I will trust in you,
Just for today
I feel you close and present,
Just for today
I remain in the moment, unafraid.
Om Sri Ram Jai Ram Jai Jai Ram

All in One

Enter gently
The inner Temple,

With pure intent
Upon the One,

Focus attention inwardly
Upon the single eye,

Stable is the mind
Drawing one step closer,

Moving deeper now
The whole attention inward,

Absorbed, absorbed
In inner space absorbed,

The Light draws one further
Guiding the way,

The Sound
Calls one to holiness,

Becoming absorbed even deeper
Into the inner stillness,

Being is vast
Being is small,

Being rests
And creates,

Being is at rest
And revelations flow,

Being is without movement
And creation bursts,

Being is without compare
And is seen as the reflection that is All,

God is Being
And I am that,

I am the I Am
Of all selves,

And all are part of the whole
And each makes up the whole,

The seed becomes the tree
And the tree becomes the seed,

And all is One
All is One,

The dreamer awakens
And knows all is One,

And One is Peace
And One is Joy,

One is Self-aware
And One knows that It knows.

Jnana-Wisdom

The development of Jnani wisdom requires the ability to focus the mind on what is unreal and what is real, separating the two and attaining the real.

Our life is the training ground for learning this wisdom. We may start our practice with our life as it is now, guiding our intellect through the maze of life's choices. The beginning of Wisdom is the recognition of the importance of the choices we make. Each choice made builds a pattern that becomes our character.

The foundation for character is the adherence, or lack of it, to the essentials of virtue. Virtue is made up of those qualities or behaviors that are known to all as positive traits. Qualities such as telling the truth, integrity, logical thinking, compassion, high-mindedness, humor, fun, etc., are those attributes that are admired in a friend, loved one, business partner, etc. Each choice we make founded upon virtue creates an engrained habit pattern—a trait that becomes who we are.

In order to identify and adhere to such virtues, we should approach with a calm mind. Some of the great minds and characters of history have, early on, developed lists of virtues they most wanted to live up to. Benjamin Franklin and George Washington both come to mind, having created lists of character virtues and actively worked at actualizing those virtues into their lives. Clear-minded values will be the guide through muddy waters of daily life where clarity in choice, temptation, and virtue can all be lost sight of in murky situations.

A lesson may be drawn from pruning bushes and trees. The first thought in pruning is what overall shape we want the plant to have. Once the overall shape is established, taking into account the nature of the plant's strengths and weaknesses, then taking away all branches not in keeping with that shape. Then one looks for all crossing branches and removes them. By this time, we have reduced all major branches to those that support the overall shape, and have removed all crossing branches. So too in our life. We determine the overall shape of virtues and values we want, remove all other branches and tendencies, then look for crossing branches; we want to encourage those daily habits that cross over the healthy branches of behavior.

There are many people of less talent and intelligence who succeed more effectively in life than their superiors, primarily because they have learned to set priorities and keep to them. Life is full of interests and fascinating aspects, but unless we narrow our focus and learn to see things through to the end, we will not achieve much success.

This ability to focus the mind and energy on positive goals and virtues is the beginning of wisdom. It is essential that we have sharp pruning instruments to cut away what is not part of our goal. Each successfully completed goal that is in keeping with the overall shape we want for our life is one more step in shaping our tree of wisdom. This includes our ventures in business, family, social circles, personal habits, marriage, children, etc. Our active spiritual life used as both nutrition and the intended fruit of our wisdom tree will make our life one of peace and joy, through all the ups and downs of worldly endeavors.

The development of wisdom in worldly life and matters becomes the tool we use for gaining spiritual wisdom as well. Our ability to identify what is within us that is not in keeping with the highest spiritual truths, the shape of our spiritual tree, and removing those branches working at cross purposes, uses skills transferred from daily behaviors inconsistent with a spiritual life to our dealing with worldly dreams and goals.

The fast, efficient use of mental discrimination cuts away all that is not of God and focuses the mind on that which is of God. The life, light, beauty, joy, and wisdom of the Superconscious mind illuminate our understanding with increased clarity as we use discrimination in our thoughts, words, and behaviors. Wisdom from the Superconscious mind is not learned but self-illuminating—Direct

Intuition replaces learned mental projections of truth. These learned laws of spirituality have their time and place, to begin with, in our journey, but with the purification of the mind, a flow of wisdom and discrimination comes naturally from hidden springs of spiritual consciousness.

The attainment of Wisdom is the spontaneous knowledge and understanding from the Superconscious mind, or the Self. As notions of a separate "I" gradually lose appeal and one can discriminate the little "I" from the Superconscious Self, God-consciousness, or the state of Being of the Eternal Self, All-consciousness and then Ever-New Bliss, becomes established.

One passes beyond the idea of the jnani, who identifies the Real from the unreal. All is perceived as part and parcel, so the real and the passing shadows of creation are known to be nothing other than the play of the Real, or God Absolute. Light, Beauty, Joy, and Freedom ring throughout all and all! All is seen to be so many movements of one undivided Life and consciousness. The Universal sports as the individual, and the individual sports with the Universal. No separation or isolation exists except where it is voluntarily assumed and clung to. Through wisdom's sharp sword of discrimination, one and all who have assumed separation may cleave to those attachments which keeps the shroud of separation intact.

What clarity and perfection come with that wisdom! An efficiency of cutting away of that which is untruth reveals Truth, the unvarnished Jewel of the Soul, resplendent in all its glory! Ah, Wisdom, servant of the wise and master of its servants, may you start us on our journey and ever illumine our way until the way and the goal unite in the perfect Wisdom of the One.

Enter In

To enter a family
Is to explore the Light and shadow
Of what it is to be human.

To enter the halls of Learning
Is to know the possibilities and limits
Of the mind.

To enter marriage
Is to learn the meaning of commitment
And to become softer of heart.

To enter parenthood
Is to experience sacrifice
And love unbounded.

To enter spiritual portages
Is to find who we truly are
And become one with the All-embracing One.

To enter old age
Is to see clearly the cycles of life
And learn the eternal youth of the heart.

To enter death
Is to leave this little human cage
And face the eternal youth of the heart.

To enter death
Is to leave this little human cage
And face what we have created.

To enter into stillness
Is to become the great I AM of Spirit
And realize we have always been that.

Detachment: The Way to Freedom and Harmony

Detachment is living in the world but not being of it. It is holding a thing without grasping it.

We have all played the game with small children. They approach us with some small object they have been carrying in their hand. When friendly contact has been made, they hand over the object. They momentarily turn their attention elsewhere, then stick their hand out, expecting us to give them the object back. And on goes the game as they experiment with the notions of possession, giving, receiving, and attachment.

Attachment is the opposite of detachment. Attachment starts with an idea. The idea is, "This is mine," or "I would like this to be mine." It is the notion of grasping, as opposed to holding. These two concepts of grasping and holding may seem to be very similar, but actually, they are worlds apart.

When we grasp something, the intention is to continue to hold the object. When the child "gives" you their object, it is done with the expectation that it will be given back to them. If we withhold it from them when they ask for it back, we will have a most unhappy child. The idea of possession and attachment is implicit in their giving and receiving. If we give the object back on demand, they may give it right back to us. But if we tease them by holding it, or if it is not their mood to give it, we find they fiercely grasp the object in their hands.

The material world tends to teach us to grasp: "Go after what you want and hold on to it!" The nature of grasping, born of attachment, is tension. Grasping is an active expenditure of mental and physical energy. Not only are we expending energy in maintaining what we have (with a background of fear that we may lose it), but we are usually in active pursuit of getting more. Of course, there is the satisfaction of winning at the game, gaining more and more, we hope, and growing in possession faster than the next fellow.

The spiritual perspective teaches us that the cost of all the grasping runs counter to spiritual awareness. The sadhaka comes to see the cost in terms of the background of fear and of loss. It is the never-ending desire nature that keeps us forever running after that elusive fulfillment and brings loss of the life-energy invested in grasping.

Yet, with all these costs, the body must be maintained, and unless we move into a cave and beg for our food, we need to have things in this world to live. So, how to do this without this notion of constant pursuit and grasping that destroys peace and spiritual awareness?

The answer is a shift of attitude more than changing our circumstances. When the child hands us the object, we may tease him or her by grasping it and not giving it back, or we may simply hold it, surrendering it on the child's demand. This shift from grasping to holding starts with a mental attitude. It gets reflected in the willful energy we project. The kind of willful energy projected gets reflected in how we physically hold the object: in tight, contracted tension or in relaxed, watchful holding.

In addition to how we hold what we have, we find that the mental attitude gets reflected in our pursuit of objects. This mental attitude has, at its most fundamental assumption, the notion of who is desiring this object. Ego consciousness, rooted in the body, says, "I want this." The spiritual attitude maintains, "I (this ego-sense of individuality) am the instrument, and God is its operator. Therefore, my thoughts, my wants, my actions are not my own, but are the result of Divine Consciousness expressing desires through me."

We cannot serve two masters; either it is God or mammon. The operator of the machine, the human mind and body, will either be seen to be God, or it will be seen as mammon. The way of seeing that it is God desiring through us does not negate that there is a higher and lower nature, and that the goal of the spiritual aspirant is the attunement with the higher nature, or God. This is the goal, in fact, of the spiritual aspirant.

However, in this dualism of lower and higher nature, it is often assumed that God has no dealings with the world at all. And this is where perceiving God's will at work, both in the spiritual and what is thought of as worldly matters, is seen in a new light. In this emerging universal vision of the sadhaka, God is known to be active at all levels of existence. There is not an area of life that is devoid of God's will or presence, nor is there any area that is devoid of the dualism of higher and lower nature that does not demand sadhakas to pay attention to their higher calling and break with their lower nature. God, being all-pervasive, prompts sadhakas in every aspect of their life.

Initially, this prompting comes from the principles or laws as enunciated by realized beings. These sometimes come to us as scripture, sometimes as the teaching of a living master or guru. Central to these teachings is the attainment of a still mind; through the stillness, the revelation of Divine Will may be received. As the allegiance of sadhakas gradually becomes focused on that inner direction, a struggle is encountered. The struggle is a result of the attachment to the body and things of this world that draws the mind out of the stillness and into the hurly-burly activity of the world. The outward focus of the mind, that is the mind glued to its own attachment to the body and the world, makes the inner focus on stillness well nigh impossible. This is why it is said that one may not serve two masters; it is to be either God or mammon. The universal laws of behavior spoken of by realized masters are guides to sadhakas to help them through the confusion created by these attachments.

If sadhakas remain sincere in their practice, the mind gradually becomes purified of its attachments. Desire for action in the world is felt to come from that inner stillness. Trial and error teach sadhakas how to distinguish between the inner peace that results from being the Divine instrument versus acting from attachment to the body.

Then all possessions are seen to be in the hold of the sadhaka, but not in his or her grasp. Like custodians for their wealthy employer, sadhakas look after all the employer's possessions with care, making sure everything is maintained perfectly. But all the while, the custodians know that none of the things watched over are theirs. Living on the premises, they use the furniture, the vehicles, and all else available to the custodians. But, at any time, the owner may say to the custodians that their time of watching after these things is up, and custodians then leave the premises without even one piece of furniture. Like custodians, sadhakas keep all the possessions in their hold, ever willing to relinquish it all at one moment's notice.

And what is the result of such a strict inner discipline? One may have vast wealth and possessions, or have very little, and in either case, the sadhaka is at peace and in perfect harmony with Divine Will. One may be in the world, but not of it—may hold possessions without grasping. With this inner detachment comes freedom and inborn wisdom. One may be a multi-billionaire, or own nothing, and both stand on equal ground. In short, through inner detachment, one can know God; no possessions can match that. No position of prestige or authority in the world can bring what knowing God brings to the sadhaka.

Detachment is the way to freedom and harmony. May you know the blessings that come with such inner freedom. May you always be in the world but not of it.

Full-Time Awareness

The goal of Life is complete God-realization. Complete God-realization is full-time awareness—it is God alone who animates this body, mind, and soul as well as every aspect of creation. This Omniscience, Omnipresence, and Omnipotence is One, without a second. When consciously realized, the body, mind, and soul are purified of any self-will directed by body-consciousness; the body is the machine and God is the operator.

The Way of achieving this complete union with God is the subject of all great religions and the teachings of realized masters. In a few rare instances this realization comes without visible preparation, complete, whole and in an instant. Other examples include brief-but-intense sadhana, others are years of intense sadhana. The length of time and the exact circumstances of a soul gaining complete realization covers a broad range and is of absorbing interest to many sadhakas.

The complexity making for this variety is partially due to the fact that souls have different starting points. It must be understood these starting points are states of mind only but may be illustrated by a physical analogy. If one were to go to New York City, the journey would be quite different depending on the starting point. If one was in New Jersey and only needed to cross a river, the way would look quite different from someone starting in Los Angeles. And for one starting from Tokyo, the way would vary even more. So too with sadhakas, depending on their makeup based on their karma, or their prior actions, the starting point, and what the path looks like will vary a great deal for aspirants.

However, all are free to start their journey at any time. It is possible for one starting in Tokyo, making a sincere, determined effort, to arrive at the destination before someone with lackluster motivation starting in New Jersey. The goal is available to all. The length of the way can vary by a wide range. The last point is that will and determination play a critical role in the success of the aspirant.

Freedom In Action: Prem-Ananda

The Guru is ever anchored in the Divine. Due to the ever-existent connection, the Guru is able to be at one with all devotees who seek shelter. The Guru may feel the devotees' pain, stand by their side as they face the dilemmas of life, and live in the devotees' hearts.

It is the devotees' sincere call that brings the Guru into their heart and soul. In their communion with God, Guru and God are one, and the devotees come to know that God has become their Guru, and Guru is ever-existent in God.

If the Guru was not thoroughly anchored in God, he or she would be caught in the whirlwind of the devotees' karma. Caught up in that whirlwind, the Guru would over-identify with disciples and lose balance. Through oneness with the Infinite, the Guru may stand with devotees through thick and thin, taking many of the karmic blows for the devotees, yet remain unaffected due to union with God.

These karmic blows may come in dark clouds of causal doubt, tortured winds of emotional turmoil, or heavy knocks to the body. Never does the Guru flinch under such conditions. Only love of the Divine, in all of its purity, can provide the mettle for the Guru. For every knock that comes, devotees may nary give a glance to the Guru and may even allow themselves to be carried off by the forces of their own karma.

What then, the fate of the Guru if he or she were attached to some outcome, expecting gratitude or understanding from the uncomprehending disciples? Would the Guru not be filled with disappointment, seeing ingratitude and worse, become bitter? Only by being anchored in the Divine, devoid of attachment, can the Guru not be swept away in separation from God.

Where then, is the source of this superhuman perspective? Why, the Guru sees it in God's expression in all nature. The sun shines on the just and the unjust the same, not withholding its life-giving rays to any. The rose wafts its fragrance to all who avail themselves of a whiff, whether they are the ones who tended the garden or neglected it. And the cedar never releases so much of its perfume as when the unmindful axe fells it to the ground.

The Guru sees countless examples in nature of how God gives without thought of reward or the merits of the receiver. Are we, who are made in the image and likeness of God, to think we should be any different?

And what reward is there for such unbounded giving? God gives through nature because it is His nature to give. To withhold would mean it would no longer have the nature of God; so, with us. We give because it is our nature to give. And for our giving to be sweet like the rose, or permeating every cell like the cedar, it must come from the heart and soul.

When giving in the spirit of God, we feel ourselves to be in union with God. We become God in action. The love and joy that permeates our being from that giving perfumes the gift with the loveliest of vibrations. If the gift is lost, unrecognized, or misused, it does not turn the gift or giver bitter. Rather the sweetness continues to permeate the air. If a perfume bottle is broken, the fragrance continues in the room more than ever. Even so, the giver of God's bounty. That beauty, love, and light going out from the giver will find its recipient.

How many saints have lived in obscurity in their own lives, only to have their sweet vibration go out and permeate all of history after them? And, how many saints faced persecution and misunderstanding only to have their influence gain in power and beauty, while others faded into obscurity? Surely, some may have thought they lived their lives in vain. How could they know that the essence of God they distilled from their own lives continued to intoxicate generations afterwards?

Saints, gurus, and devotees have hearts that beat with the same light. The essence of what they distill from life will leave its imprint on all those who follow. Whether it be the vibration of Jesus or

Judas, Rama or Ravana, the effect of how a life is lived exists long after the physical life is gone. Whether it be of the famous or the obscure, each leave their print. Could the famous have lived their lives if not for the sacrifice of countless ones playing their parts in obscurity?

Each one of us has a part to play. As in a theatrical production, a minor part may turn out to be the star performance when played to perfection. There are no minor parts, for each must play their part well to make the play great.

The greatest way to play our part in this Divine drama is to anchor ourselves to the Divine, then we play the part with all our heart and soul. We do not hold back, neither do we become attached. Bliss comes from knowing we are the Divine playing the role. We give without thought of reward; we act for the sake of the role assigned. We remain in freedom even amidst activity.

O Sadhaka! This is our time on the stage. Let us savor our role, but never forget our Divine heritage. We are God in human form, here to fulfill a sacred purpose, even in mundane activities. All come from Ananda, Bliss; all return to Ananda. And when looked at through the lens of God's Light, all is love—our eternal treasures, attributes. Prem Ananda, Love and Bliss. May all sadhakas ever be filled with Prem Ananda, now and always!

Flowers of My Dreams

The flowers of my dreams
Are blooming on my altar for Thee,
For Thou hast seen my piteous cries
And bent Yourself to lift me up.

Who can say how sweet Your sweetness is?
Who can tell of Your glorious mantle white?
Who can serve as they ought to serve

The Light of unspeakable Beauty You are?

Fathomless is the love I feel for You, my Lord,
Breathless is my adoration at Your Feet.
Why? Because touching You I feel Your Nature
Breathing in, I taste Your nectar Presence.

And, in touching You, tasting You,
My Soul melts into Your Being
And naturally so, for Your lover,
I feel myself spreading over Your
Fathomless breathless nature.

A Nature so vast, no bird could wing,
A Beauty so rapturous, no artist could paint,
A Compassionate Empathy, no saint could ever tell,
A Love indescribable, no earthly love could approximate.

I die—I die in my Soul into Your Being!
And as I do, You are writing these very words with Your own hand.
Your love breaks this tiny human heart
Into a million prisms of Light that continue
To sing Your Name evermore.

The Guru's Glory is God's Glory

The Guru's glory is God's glory. To surrender to the Guru brings his or her mantle down upon us: it is the mantle of light, purity, and love. The Guru's mantle is God Itself. What is beyond good and evil? God alone—His love, light, and all-knowing wisdom. With compassion and equality, God sees all His creation as original innocence, because He is original innocence itself. Every body is a temple of light and purity to the all-comprehending intelligence of God. When we see creation as God does, we shall be as God: all bliss, ever-new joy, in peace, and with unerring wisdom and equal vision.

The word of God is not stale, stagnant, or old fashioned. If we think so, the error is ours, not God's. God is you, me, and this entire creation. In fact, God is not only this fascinating creation but is the unlimited potential beyond it as well. I say, "Don't find a new word for God; change your understanding to match the grandeur that is God!"

God is your Friend of friends. He resides in your heart. God is not man, woman, or any other thing. God is the life and intelligence that gives you the power to live, breathe, move, think—everything is done by that power and intelligence. God is not far off, but is the breath behind your breath, the feeling behind your feeling, the thought behind your thought. Eliminate all ideas of separation now! And God is yours.

Freedom, real freedom, is not the capacity to do anything you want. Real freedom is the result of self-mastery. Self-mastery results in total surrender. Total surrender brings about the annihilation of the ego-self. Annihilation of the ego-self produces a rebirth in God-consciousness, and that is real, absolute freedom.

Recognize the sole power of God as humility. When I first started giving talks at my Guru's request, I was subject to other people's projections, as they saw in me what was actually in themselves. A spouse of one of the devotees said, "You must feel real power when you give talks." His comment made me feel soiled, unclean. Yes, I felt the power of God flow through me; no other experience compares to that. But it is not an ego thing of feeling powerful. It is the complete reliance on God and feeling His power and intelligence acting through me.

Another situation came about when I first gave talks. People would come up to me and say, "I saw Master (or Mother) in your place while you were talking." Of course, it is wonderful to think the Masters are near. One woman who thought of herself as highly advanced once commented after a talk, "I saw all the Masters on either side of you when you were speaking." God prompted me to reply, "That is a reflection of your own consciousness." She was quite vain, and said, "Yes, yes that is true." And I saw her ego take in everything. It is a fascinating play.

When I meet people, I immediately see their state of mind. Whether they feel guided in uplifted states of mind, or they can be leading an immoral life headed for trouble, it is all written on their brow.

I do not comment on most people's development. Sometimes I build their ego a bit because they are in need of a boost; sometimes, I ignore them because they need their wings of ego clipped a bit. The Infinite does it all; I am merely the machine. God is the operator. He does all, for the highest good of all.

As I have grown, I have become more direct. It is an art to be direct without being blunt. Some people are blunt and say they are only speaking the truth. But it is not really truth; they are speaking because their motives are not pure. One must have pure motives to speak the truth; otherwise, what they say may be factually true but built on a lie.

God is purity itself. To realize God, you must be pure, but if you are filled with the impurity of the ego, only God can make you pure. Only Grace can be your salvation.

God-realization is not seeing or hearing something in a vision. God-realization must be the total transformation. You do not become someone else, but, for the first time, you truly become yourself.

Having outer purity without the corresponding inner purity is hypocrisy. Love of God, of truth, and desire for realization must outshine desire for the things of the body or the world. Without that burning desire, you will not achieve your goal of realization.

The Seed that Yields Fruits

O Sadhaka
Long does the Master wish to share,
Share the wealth of Its heart and soul
The super abundant share of Its Spirit.
It longs for you to receive
To receive all It has to give
But a full pitcher cannot receive

Only when it is empty may it be receptive.
O Sadhaka
Open your heart and mind
Rid it of the contents of the world,
And like an opening bud become
The glorious warmth of morning Light.
Open yourselves to quiet yearning
Experientially awaiting the glance of inner Light,
Patiently be that expectancy
For it is not given to the over-anxious.

O Sadhaka
The opening is yours,
The Day is ripe for harvest
Of seed that yields such glorious fruits.

The Mystic Light Within

Feel that mystic Light within you. You may live in the city, dress in normal fashion, but in your heart beats the same Light that animates yogis of Himalayan peaks and the desert prophets of old. You do not need to be of the desert or the mountains to know what they know, to feel what they feel. Turn your mind to the same Source of life, purity of Spirit and Light of Being they focus upon.

That Light is in your heart; it is not far away but as close as your breath!

True knowledge does not come from books or lectures. True knowledge comes from the crucible of experience. It is in this crucible that you strive, yearn, and work for the impossible. It is impossible, but for the ingredient of grace. Grace is the all-powerful force within you that transcends your doubt, weakness, and ignorance. The crucible produces heat, pressure; it dissembles and rearranges the atoms of your being. Do you think that kind of change comes with just some passing interest? Passionate yearning for Truth, Freedom, and Light must take hold of your whole self. This kind of yearning is a result of Grace. You can open yourself to that Grace by praying for it. When you create an opening, then Grace will fill you up and make the cauldron crucible to boil, producing in you a Divine Being.

This life in God is like no other; it demands all from you, physically, mentally, and spiritually. This life in God will take what you give and transmute it from dross to the gold of Spirit. It demands your all, but it gives back so much more.

Scriptures like the Bhagavad Gita and the Sermon on the Mount do not appear out of thin air. These sayings are the distilled wisdom of intense practice, yielding a profound wisdom. Who can understand the power behind these words that has inspired God-men and women for thousands of years? Twenty or thirty years of meditative study will certainly result in priceless gems of realization. But to say one has encompassed the depth of these scriptures would be tantamount to saying one has circumscribed God! Use the scriptures as guides to take you deeper until you become a creature of the Deep. Even then, these glowing words will move you as no others can.

There are many today who object to the notion of religion or God. Instead, they talk of spirituality and the Self, or nirvana. This distinction is, in reality, artificial. There are those of orthodox minds in every religion. Their mind-set is concrete. They tend to think they are right and all others are wrong. This is as true of those who speak of religion as it is of those who speak of spirituality. It is a form of ignorance and pride.

God does not care about what name He is called, or whether the reference is to a He, She, or It. God looks to the heart. If the heart is sincere, soft, and yearning, God is pleased. If the heart is full of pride, ignorance, and I, me, and mine, He becomes a stranger. It is not a matter of education, which religion one belongs to, or even a belief system. It is a matter of the attitude of the heart.

Krishna, speaking as the Infinite, says, "I do not care what you offer me, it can be a leaf, a drop of water, anything offered with a sincere heart is acceptable to Me." (Gita 9:26) You see, God looks into the heart. A great devotee said, "And if I am wandering about and do not even have a drop of water, what then?" Krishna replied, "As long as you have even one drop of water in your eye as a tear for me, I consider that a more valuable gift than gold, jewels, or money given by others!"

So, you can take all artificial divisions and throw them into the ocean. Speak to God with your heart, no matter what name or mental concept, as long as it pleases you and purifies your heart. Those with a pure heart shall see God.

There are many teachings and techniques you can use to get over interior hurdles. They are given to be of help. Like a craftsman uses tools to create something beautiful, when the project is done, the tools are put away. Even so, the spiritual techniques; when God is realized, the techniques are no longer needed. Some would-be craftsmen collect many tools, but remain unskilled in their use. So, it is with many would-be spiritual aspirants. They read books, listen to lectures, but refrain from real, deepened practice. Only those who sincerely practice will make progress towards the goal.

It is time to put away artificial divisions made in God. All religions strive for the same ultimate goal, to bridge the gap between individual humans and God. Through love, support, and understanding, you will come to see there are many sincere devotees in every religion the world over. This universal recognition will help heal divisions among people, and therefore help heal the division between individual humans and God. With love, faith, and sincerity, may all live according to their highest creed and attain their goal.

O Mighty Spirit

O Mighty Supreme Spirit
I pray that all souls may
Manifest Thy Light and Purity.

O Omnipotent force
You have created all;
Awaken Thy children
So that all may live in harmony
With Thy perfect will of peace and joy.

Scale Beyond the Peak

God is not religion. Religions are so many approaches to scaling the mountain of God. Most often, religion sets up a station at some distance, but within sight of the mountain, and says, "Worship God from here, safe within our compound."

But the realized ones have scaled the mountainside. From viewpoints along the way come poems, music, and scriptures, describing vistas that move and inspire the soul. Some souls climb so far and no more. Some climb to a certain height, then descend to set up a temple of worship, saying that this temple is purer than the other temple-religions already established.

Some souls are busy climbing to the top, and simply disappear into the blue-sky clad ceiling above the mountain. A few souls climb to the top, and through inspiration, guide others to scale those peaks. They inspire others to transcend the many false peaks, and furthermore, to continue on to their emancipation at the summit of the All in All.

What is required to scale the mountain that is God? The first requirement is sincerity, without it nothing of real value can be done. The next attribute is an all-consuming desire for the peak; nothing less will do. The third necessity is to have a way-shower, one who has been there, and can make the journey possible for the aspirant. Finally, what is needed is a willingness to give life and limb in the ascent, and to never give up, to never give in!

If individuals look deeply, they will discover these attributes within, and will overcome every obstacle encountered along the way. The path is strewn with aborted attempts from those who had too little of what is essential. However, aborted attempts are not lost expenditures of effort. Those climbers will one day resume their climb, and the lessons learned from mistakes made will be deeply ingrained these individuals. Let us look at those vain attempts without haughtiness, lest we fall into a deep crevice ourselves. Rather, let us draw deeply from a lesson well learned by the example of another. Pride will blind us to the right choices; arrogance leads to misperception. But also, do not be dismayed by apparent difficulty. Our Guide will see to it that our sincere effort will find fulfillment. Be of good cheer! Those who follow their Guru-guide, placing one foot in front of the other, will scale to that peak—keep your eyes ever glued on it, and your footsteps will naturally lead you closer.

At first, you may have to traverse through the trees of wilderness and only catch occasional glimpses of the peak. But then you transcend the treeline and have continuous vision of the peak. This however, is not the end of your journey. Continue up, moving beyond the beyond. Then is God seen without limit as the All in All. Be not afraid, but tread on and on, and the goal must surely be yours.

Affirmation for Meditation...

I am a loving child of God;
Rich ideas from God are now pouring into my consciousness.
God gives me dominion over fear, hate, weakness, and poverty.
In harmony,
I am continually protected by God's love.
Disturbances cannot annoy me, because I abide in God's presence.
Through the help of God, I am master of my emotions.
No disappointment can disturb or discourage me.

OM TAT SAT

Yogacharya David

APPENDIX 1

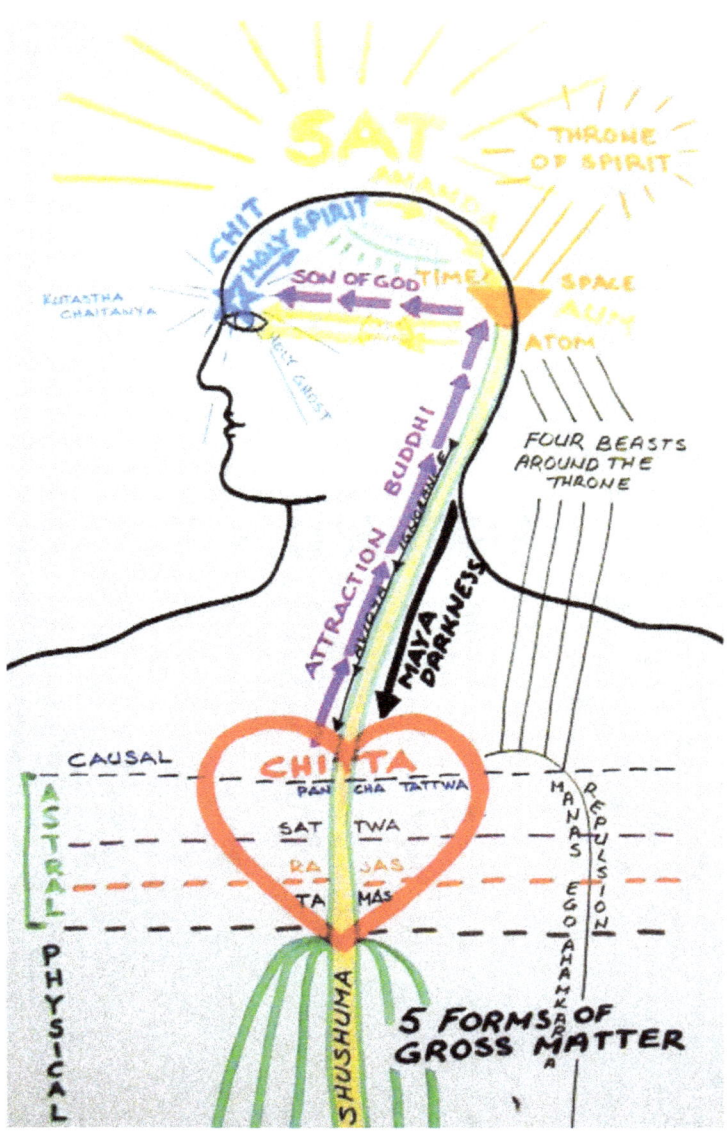

The Cosmic Human

THE TWENTY-FOUR ASPECTS OF CREATION

Introduction

This addendum is my companion to a portrait of "The Cosmic Man." This drawing is inspired by Sri Yukteswar's description in *The Holy Science* of the creation of the cosmos. As the microcosm of man is designed as a reflection of the macrocosm of all creation, nay, even of God Itself, I have applied the various aspects of Sri Yukteswar's delineation of all creation to that of the inner cosmic man. This may give a deepened appreciation for this wonderful body temple—the temple not made with hands. Not only an appreciation for its remarkable design, but its ultimate potential to become a worthy temple of worship, that is a place of realization.

I have numbered twenty-four aspects to Sri Yukteswar's account, to be found in Chapter One of *The Holy Science*.[1] This should not be confused with his twenty-four principles he enunciates in his commentary on the scriptures, both of East and West. This correspondence of numbers came about as a synchronicity after I had drawn the portrait and then decided to add this companion writing with numbers. You will note my twenty-four aspects begin with Sat, that which is formless, beginningless, and endless. Sri Yukteswar's twenty-four principles represent the formation of creation after the effects of the ideas of time, space, and atom.

The creation of this picture and companion writing was done over a couple of days at a feverish pace, as if it could not be completed soon enough. As with all occurrences these days, I feel it was done through me, not coming, or originating, from me. I am

---

1   *The Holy Science* by Jnanavatar Swami Sriyuktewsar Giri, Chapter 1, Sutra 2, published by Yogoda Sat-Sanga Society of India, 3rd Edition, 1949.

aware that Divine Intelligence is perfect, pure, and complete unto itself. Whatever errors are inherent are due to the limitation of the human instrument. I say inherent because human instruments will always express some apparent flaw. The greater the purity of the consciousness of the instrument, the closer will be the approximation to the original purity of Divine Consciousness.

The fact that any truth expressed comes through a human mind, no matter how purified, and the fact that it is received through a human mind, require that it will never represent absolute Truth. The greatest work an expressed truth will generate will be for the inspiration and guidance provided to bring questing souls to their own direct perception of Truth, which resides beyond the mind. This is my wish for you: as you read, think about, absorb, and realize the great potential that man is, being a Son of God.

I have added a number of quotes from the Bible, particularly from Genesis, that will add appreciation for those ancient scripts and a sense of wonder at their close approximations to their Hindu cousins. At the time of this writing, my body feeling the strain of inflexible creative flow of the last few days, I bow down in gratitude to Sri Yukteswar and the great spiritual Masters, both East and West.

Those who are granted views from places on high stand on the shoulders of these great spiritual giants. May you be blessed, as they were so obviously blessed, to realize your inherent oneness with Sat Chid Ananda and ever reside in the consciousness of the Son of God.

Twenty-Four Aspects of Creation

Sutra 1

Aspect 1

SAT: Eternal Father: the only Real Substance. Sat is one, without a second. It is without form, beginningless and endless. It is unknowable by the intellect, and resides beyond all creation; yet, it is the very Substance from which all of creation is created.

> Hear O Israel, the Lord our God is one Lord. (Deuteronomy 6:4)

> In the Beginning, God created heaven and earth. And the earth was without form and void, and darkness was upon the face of the deep. (Genesis 1:12)

Sutra 2

Aspect 2

CHIT (also CHID): Omniscient feeling makes the world conscious; it is the source of Divine Love and Light.

> And the Spirit of God moved upon the waters (consciousness). And God said, Let there be Light: and there was Light. (Genesis 1:2–3)

Aspect 3

ANANDA: Eternal Joy: Shakti, Almighty Force, that produces the world.[2]

---

2   *The Holy Science* originally states Ananda (Eternal Joy) *produces* this world; editors later changed this to *produced*.

> Let there be a firmament in the midst of the waters, and let it divide the waters from the waters (the idea of separation required for creation)... and God called the firmament Heaven... and God said, Let the waters under heaven be gathered together in one place, and let the dry land appear (the idea of physical creation)... and God called the dry land Earth. (Genesis 1:6–10)

Aspect 4

Prakriti: Chid and Ananda together demonstrate the Nature (Prakriti) of God the Father (Sat).

> And God made the firmament (Light of heaven, Chid), and divided the waters (through the Shakti of Ananda) which were under the firmament (of a lower vibration rate) from the waters which were above the firmament (Sat nature of God): and it was so. (Genesis 1:7)

Sutra 3

Aspect 5

Aum: The manifestation of Prakriti is the vibration of Aum, Amen (the Word). It comes as the sound vibration of all creation.

> These things saith the Amen, the faithful and true witness, the beginning of the creation of God. (John 1:1–3)

> And Aum, the Word, manifests as:

Aspect 6

Desa: the idea of division.

> And God divided the Light from the darkness. (Genesis 1:4) And God said Let there be a firmament in the midst

of the waters, and let it divide the waters from the waters. And God made the firmament, and divided the waters which were under the firmament from the waters which were above the firmament (Genesis 1:6–7) and called the dry land Earth; and the gathering of the waters, seas (Genesis 1:10) and God said Let the earth bring forth grass, the herb yielding seed, and the fruit tree yielding fruit after his kind, whose seed is in itself (multiplicity through division after division of that which is indivisible Substance is made possible by Maya). (Genesis 1:11)

Aspect 7
Kala: idea of change.

> And God said, Let there be Lights in the firmament of heaven to divide the day from the night; and let them be for signs, and for seasons, and for days and years. (Genesis 1:11)

The ensuing effect is:

Aspect 8
Anu: the idea of particles—Innumerable atoms.

> And God said, Let the waters under heaven be gathered together (density of mass) unto one place (material creation) and let the dry land appear. (Genesis1: 9)

The Word (Aum, Amen), time (Kala), Space (Desa), and the atom (Anu) are the four ideas projected by the Eternal Father (Sat) through Mother Nature (Prakriti). The Aum vibration of the Word resonates with the highest vibrational nature of God, Sat. Therefore, it can be said that the Word (Aum) and God are one. The analogies often quoted are: just as fire and its burning power cannot be separated, and, just as the substance of milk and its color of white cannot be separated, so God (as formless Spirit) and His creation (God with form through Aum) are inseparable.

Sutra 4

Aspect 9
Throne of Spirit: Aum, Kala, Desa, and Anu make up the throne of Spirit. The Creator shining upon this Throne creates this universe.

> And immediately I was in the Spirit (raised in high consciousness): and behold (through inner vision), a throne was set in heaven (a revelation of the creative forces became clear in high spiritual vibration). (Revelation 4:2)

Aspect 10
Maya: These four ideas of the throne, which are represented by the idea that atoms beget creation, which in total create Maya, the darkness, as they delude the senses into thinking creation is absolute reality, keeping the individual from comprehending, or realizing, the great Light of God's Being.

> And God said Let there be light (of Chid nature), and there was Light (feeling consciousness). And God saw that it was good (an uplifting vibration): And God divided the Light from the darkness (lower creative vibration). And God called the Light day (enlightenment). And the darkness he called night (uncomprehending of Truth, Light, the Real Substance of creation). (Genesis 1:3–4)

Aspect 11
Avidya is the individual atom that creates ignorance, as it makes man ignorant of his own Self.

In him (the Word) was life; and the Life was the Light
of men. And the Light shineth in the darkness; and the
darkness comprehended it not. (John 1:3–5)

Aspect 12

Four Beasts in the midst and around the throne: When man identifies with body consciousness: i.e., the darkness of Maya and the
ignorance of Avidya, the mind is confused with the seemingly final
realities of time, space, and materiality built of atoms. These illu-
sionary ideas emanate from the Aum power vibration and inter-
fere with the deluded mind's ability to comprehend the primordial
Light of God. Therefore, these four creative principles are pictured
as four beasts around the Throne of Spirit when seen from manas,
sense-deluded mind. In his revelatory vision, St. John the Divine
sees the true nature of this reality as omniscient, simultaneously
seeing before and behind.

And in the midst of the throne, and round about the
throne, were four beasts full of eyes before and behind.
(Revelation 4:6)

Sutra 5

Aspect 13

Kutastha Chaitanya: Omniscient love (Chid) manifests as the Self.
Kutastha Chaitanya (centered in the body at the ajna) is the power
of attraction of love, which is the power of God Itself. It is the savior aspect sown throughout all creation. This Light that draws all
to SAT, God the Father, may be seen at the ajna, the third eye point.

The Light of the body is the eye: if therefore thine eye
be single, thy whole body shall be filled with light. But

> if thine eye be evil (Avidya or ignorance consciousness), thy whole body shall be full of darkness (perceiving only delusive Maya). If therefore the light that is in thee be darkness, how great is that darkness! (The Consciousness is filled with confusion, error, separation, and ignorance of tamas. How very true to call this state a great darkness!). (Matthew 6:22–23)

Aspect 14

The Holy Ghost: The Omniscient love of the Kutastha Chaitanya shines out to all creation (as the Holy Ghost), calling its children home. But the children are full of Avidya, ignorance, and do not care for the Light. They reject the light that is constantly shining upon them.

> That was the true Light which lighteth every man that cometh into the world. He (the Light) was in the world, and the world was made by him, and the world knew him not. He came unto his own, and his own received him not. (John 1:9–11)

Aspect 15

Son of God: When man accepts this light, is able to comprehend it through Self- realization, and is attracted by the love of universal Nature, he becomes a Son of God, Purusha.[3]

> But as many received him, to them gave he power to become the Sons of God, even to them that believe on his name (are uplifted on the sound current of Aum, Amen): which were born not of blood, nor of the will of flesh, nor

---

3   In Sankya Philosophy, Purusha is the capital "S" of Self. In other Indian philosophies, purusha is a lower-case "p," and will translate to mean man, or the animating principle in man. Sri Yukteswar draws from the analytical Sankya meaning.

of the will of man, but of God (drawn up by the Grace of Divine love and reborn in the light of the Kutastha Chaitanya, Christ Consciousness). (John 1:12–13)

Sutra 6

Aspect 16

Chitta: This atom (Avidya, individualized ignorance), under the influence of Chid, universal love, creates a spiritualized field, like a magnet aura, whereby the atom becomes conscious with the power of feeling. This is called Chitta (the calm state of mind). And like a magnet, Chitta has a positive and negative pole. The positive pole takes on the quality of Chid, the magnetic drawing power of Divine Love. The negative pole is repulsion to the light and continues the outward, or downward, journey of the atom of ignorance and darkness.

Aspect 17

Buddhi: The positive pole of Chitta, when spiritually oriented, becomes Buddhi, or Sattva, discriminative Intelligence. With Buddhi, the individual can determine Truth, the Real, Sat (God the Father) from the unreal (ignorance and darkness) and is drawn up by Divine Love.

Aspect 18

Manas: The negative pole of Chitta has repulsion to the Light and manifests as Manas, drawn to ananda (lower-case "a"), enjoyment of the senses.

Aspect 19

Ego: It is in Manas, the sense-oriented mind, that jiva, the self, is formed with Ahamkara, the ego, the idea of separate existence.

> And God made two great lights: the greater Light (the sun of Kutastha Chaitanya, centered in the ajna) to rule the day (Buddhi that brings the light of discernment) and the lesser Light (solar plexus, human intuition, the moon or second sun center) to rule night (to guide manas through intuition while under the influence of darkness, Maya, and ignorance, Avidya). (Genesis 1:16)

Sutras 7–10

Aspect 20

Pancha Tattwa: (Pancha: five, Tattwa: aura, electricity, or principles.) The Chitta, the spiritualized Atom of the heart, produces five different sorts of aura electricities as the Causal Body. These five electricities,[4] being under the influence of the Holy Ghost, drawing them to Sat, produce a magnetic field of Sattva Buddhi, the Intelligence. These five ideas create the body of the Causal Being, the Purusha or Son of God.

> And God said, Let the waters (consciousness) bring forth abundantly the moving creature (that which allows for movement, or a body: the primal body of Causal Man), that hath life (electricity ideas or the principles that make up the body), and fowl (higher-flown thought forms) that may fly above the earth (resides beyond the material mind) in the open firmament (the *firmament* is the astral heaven and the *open firmament* goes beyond the astral to the Causal Realm). (Genesis 1:20)

---

4   The number 5 is a recurring theme for man: five senses, five fingers per hand, five toes per foot, and when man stands upright with his feet apart, arms outstretched, and head erect, he is in the form of a five-pointed star. These physical attributes have their root cause in the Pancha Tattwa. The five-pointed star of Christ Consciousness, beheld at the Kutastha Chaitanya, leads man back to pure causal consciousness. By going through the star, man ascends to Sat, God the Father.

Aspect 21–23
The Astral Body: Made of the five electricities (idea principles) drawn from the Causal Realm or body. At this point, the three Gunas come into manifestation. The three Gunas are sattva (positive), rajas (neutral), and tamas (negative).[5]

Aspect 21
Sattva: The positive attributes of the five electricities are Jnanendriyas (the organs of sense for both astral and physical experience, these make up the body of Manas.)

Aspect 22
Rajas: The neutralizing attributes of the five electricities are the organs of action (Karmendriyas). These organs allow for excretion, generation, speech, motion (feet), and manual skill (hands). These electricities make up the energetic body (prana) from the heart.

Aspect 23
Tamas: The negative attributes of the five electricities are the objects of the senses and when united with the organs of sense (rajasic organs of action), they satisfy the desires of the heart (for sensory life). This completes the astral body.

> And God created great whales (under water is the subconscious mind repository of Tamasic qualities, the original word in Genesis also meant sea monsters and dragons)...and every winged fowl (birds are lofty thoughts of sattvic qualities)...And God said, let the

---

5   Sri Yukteswar again uses Sankya designations for the Gunas that may vary from other definitions you have heard. There are six main philosophical systems in India, Sankya being one of them. These philosophies share many words but give differing definitions. (Fortunately, becoming realized does not require mastering all six philosophical systems!) These scriptural interpretations are meant to orient the mind to the true purpose of life: the realization of God as Sat Chid Ananda.

earth bring forth the living creature after his kind (earth is neutralizing rajasic qualities). (Genesis 1:21–24)

Sutras 11, 12

Aspect 24
Five Forms of Gross Matter: The five tamasic electricities of the astral body combined together produce the idea of gross matter, which appear to us in five varieties: The solid (Kshiti), the Liquid (Ap), the fiery (Tejas), the gaseous (Marut), and the ethereal (Akasa or Vyona).

> And God said let us make man in our image (according to the creative principles just enunciated), after our likeness (having his origins in Sat, unmanifested Spirit): and let him have domain over fish of the sea (self-mastery of the subconscious mind), and over fowl of the air (higher intelligence), and over cattle, and over all the earth, and over every creeping thing upon the earth (self-mastery over the body consciousness and the subtle astral and causal bodies. Guided by the twin Lights of Divine Christ Consciousness of the ajna and human intuition of the solar plexus (the second sun), man was designed to live free in harmony with nature and Spirit through the guidance of intuition at the solar plexus and the wisdom Light at the ajna). (Genesis 1:26)

Summary: This completes the 24 Principles that clothe the Son of God (Purusha), in Its various bodies. They are:

1. Chitta: Intelligent Consciousness, power of feeling
2. Buddhi: Discriminative intelligence
3. Manas: Sense Mind
4. Ahamkara: Ego

5–9.   Jnanendriyas: Five instruments of sense perception

10–14.   Karmendriyas: Five instruments of action

15–19.   Tanmatras: Five objects of the senses: smell, taste, sight, touch, and sound

20–24.   Gross matter: Five ideas of gross matter.

> And around about the throne were four and twenty seats; and upon the seats I saw four and twenty elders. (Revelation 4:4)

Creation comes about as a projected idea from Sat, brought to conscious awareness through Chid, and into being through the Blissful vibratory power of Ananda. God assumes a mask, then divides into innumerable forms for His masquerade play, His lila. We are meant always to remember our Divine origin and not become attached to the ephemeral creation. This attachment creates identification with the forces of duality and causes misery and suffering.

> And the lord God commanded the man, saying, Of every tree of the garden thou mayest freely eat (all vibratory creation is good to experience and does not bind the soul): But of the tree of the knowledge of good and evil (duality consciousness), thou shalt not eat of it (not identify with duality): for in the day that thou eatest (bring the idea in for consumption), thou shalt surely die (will enter into realms of birth and death and through that identification, create suffering for yourself by forgetting your Divine origins). (Genesis 2:16–17)

God's essential Nature is Bliss (Ananda), Conscious Awareness (Chid), and knowledge of the Eternal Self (Sat). By reestablishing our consciousness in Him (realizing our Sat-nature or His likeness), we establish the correct relationship with creation (His image). We once again are seated on the throne of Supreme Consciousness.

> To him that overcometh (raises life-force to Christ Consciousness) will I grant to sit with me in my throne (reside in Christ Consciousness), even as I overcame (gained self-mastery and surrendered all) and am set down with my Father in His throne (in Christ Consciousness one rises to know Sat Consciousness as well). He that hath an ear (one who has receptive consciousness), let him hear what the Spirit saith unto the churches (open that receptivity to the vibratory power that awakens the "churches" of all the chakras). (Revelation 3: 21–22) (From 2001 version.)

> Behold, I stand at the door (the ajna) and knock (the sound of Aum, Amen at the medulla): if any man hear my voice (the Aum), and open the door (enter through the ajna into Light of Chit), I will come in to him (the soul will be uplifted into Christ Consciousness) and will sup with him, and he with me (the individual soul will be in communion with Christ Consciousness). To him that overcometh (gains self-mastery and withdraws life-force up the spine to the ajna) will I grant to sit by me in my throne (become established in Christ Consciousness), even as I also overcame (gained complete self-mastery and surrender), and am sat down (no longer struggling i.e., in a natural state) with my Father in His Throne (Christ Consciousness merges with Sat Consciousness in Sahaja Samadhi). He that hath an ear (one who has receptive attunement), let him hear what the Spirit saith unto the churches (experience the Aum vibration awakening the

chakras to higher spiritual Consciousness). (Revelation 3:20–22) (From 2018 version.)

This creation was meant for soul enjoyment and experience while remaining one with the Father, Sat-Consciousness. May you be awakened to the real Nature of your Father God and become established in Sat Chid Ananda, forever and ever! Aum-en.

... And God saw everything that he had made, and behold, it was very good. (Genesis 1:31)

APPENDIX 2

CREATION STORY

I am going to tell you a story of Creation.

In the beginning, God was. Of course, there was not really a beginning because God is beyond time, but we have to use that kind of language in order for it to make sense to us. Anyway, as I say, in the beginning, God was. God was complete, whole, one without a second.

Then the creative juices in God thought up a play, a wonderful drama to express Himself. Why create? Because it is His Nature to create, that's why. He thought to Himself (He could only think to Himself since there was no other), "Wouldn't it be fun to create scenery and characters that are not omnisciently aware at all times? These characters, who are none other than Myself, since there is no other, can carry on operating through limited sense perception, growing and developing along individual lines. Let's just see where My mind takes Me in creating all of this."

So quick as a thought, God (Sat) projected out lovely stage lighting (Chid) so He could see what He was doing. Then He made a joy-filled backdrop screen (Ananda/Prakriti) for contrast. On that backdrop, God got busy and one could hear the sound (Aum) of further construction. Up popped a stage, creating a space (Desa), and then a really unique creation that allowed for a sequence of events called time (Kala). Oh, God was really pleased with this beginning and was having so much fun, and exclaimed, "This is Good!"

The show, God's lila, was really starting to get interesting, and He was most fascinated to see what He would dream up next! Suddenly, a large vibrational sound (Aum) could be heard, stage left. Particles (Anu) streamed onto the stage (Maya). At first, it did not look like much, but then in a sudden burst of thought (Causal), the particles exploded like fireworks in the sky; all exclaimed in thrills of ooohs and aaahs. A big bright explosion of Light, looking like a large colorful balloon (Astral Worlds), formed into gorgeous expanses of galaxies, stars, and planets. Oh, what variety and beauty, this was getting better all the time!

Now different ones emerged out of the whole as individual points of consciousness (jivas or souls), thinking they too would like to create. These Causal Beings were a combination of producers and screenwriters for the play, the idea people. Others wanted to be directors and actors for the play and dove right into the action as Astral Beings. As quick as a thought, they projected themselves into the dream creation of the Astral Worlds, which became teeming with life. They donned costumes of various forms and learned to operate the sense controls, moving pieces of the sets around and interacting with others doing the same. Oh, the joy, fun, and love of it all were wonderful.

God then thought to Himself, "All are having such a great time acting, having control of the sets, and playing their individual roles. What more can I do? Hmmmm? I know, let's slow down the rate of vibration of the particles, making it different from the bright balloon of the Astral Worlds, thus making the particles denser, more like molasses."

"Hmmm, what is molasses?"

"Don't know, have yet to think that up. I will figure that out as I go along." (God talks to Himself like that, probably a product of spending too much time with Himself!)

On stage left again was heard a deep rumbling sound. A stream of different particles other than the Astral World came onto the stage. Well, this new development had the attention of the audience, writers, and actors. What in the world was going to happen now?! The deep rumbling grew louder and with a sudden bang! (That made everyone jump in delight.) A much smaller, denser Material Creation came about. All felt Joy and Love as they gazed on this new arrival; much darker than the balloon, it hung like a dense basket under the colorful balloon.

What marvels might there be next, they wondered? The actors in the Astral balloon were especially intrigued about the Material

Creation since they were having so much fun in the Astral. God said to all:

> Ok, here's the deal. If you go into this new creation, the Material World, it has some unusual properties. I made this creation an even more complex maze than you have seen before. If, in your sojourn there, you stay focused on your connection with Me, you can get out anytime you want. But! If you identify with your character while there, you will become lost (Avidya) in the maze (Maya). Now, of course, in reality, you are never really separate from Me, but if you identify with your character in the maze, you will forget Me. This is a much denser world, so it is harder to move and there are not as many control options. However, I think many of you will find it a very interesting challenge to enter this maze and then find your way back out. Like all creation, what you experience is really a projection of your own thoughts.

Some stood back, not sure they wanted anything to do with this darker, less free Material World. Others had their curiosity aroused and looked deeper into this dark maze, fascinated at the challenge of finding their way through it. Some thought, "What if I get lost? But did the Creator not say I could never really be separate from Him, it was all a projection of my own thoughts?"

As the creative "Bang" started to coalesce, there appeared some interesting prospects. "Oh, there is a planet forming now! Watch as it all comes together, isn't it fascinating and beautiful?" Losing any inhibition, gazing at the forming planet, wondering what it would be like to experience oneself as flowing red-hot lava rock, the soul, quick as a thought, merged into that projected creation.

"Oh, isn't this interesting? Flowing from mountain to sea as molten rock, hardening now, feeling the pressure of other rock pushing against me. Ahhh." And so, the play proceeds. When one is done exploring the idea of being mineral, the mineral idea falls away like an outer sheath revealing a new life as vegetation. When the soul is done exploring vegetation, another sheath falls away and reveals the freedom of movement as animal. And when done exploring animal, that sheath layer falls away to reveal human. Working from one maze to another, mineral, vegetable, animal, and then human, the course is run.

Through each successive layer, an unconscious principle prompts the soul to become more conscious of the various levels of Material Creation. Maze after maze presents itself, going deeper into identification with these strange, fascinating, and mysterious creations. An unconscious drive leads the soul on and on, all the while a certain feeling of connection with the Creator is always in the background. At last, the soul knows what it is to be human.

At first, the human incarnation is much like the animal. Instinct and conditioning form most of the behavioral patterns. The animal mind (manas) is rooted in body consciousness and its immediate surroundings. It is rough play, but all the while, the soul feels committed to working its way through the maze. Through successive human births, the brain and capacity for higher thought develop. The higher-functioning mind (Buddhi) is at first focused on solving human dilemmas. Unlike the animal, humans are self-aware. Through that self-awareness, they think more about their world and its creative possibilities. Rules of conduct, organization, and modes of worship begin to take shape.

When animal instinct dominates the human's thinking, the idea of "I," "me" and "mine" are limited in scope. With this higher-functioning mind, those ideas become more developed. The mind recognizes the notion of free will and the consequences of choice. The play for the soul gets even more complex and interesting at this time. Higher thought leads to more experimentation than before. Deeds not even considered to this point, now have an allure. Sensual, delightful, soul-forgetting joys and worldly ambitions look interesting. But somewhere, deeply embedded in the consciousness, is a warning signal. It is telling the soul, "No, don't go there! If you do, you will lose all connection with Me!" The signal keeps sounding, but… "Wouldn't it be nice to try? It couldn't hurt to try."

The idea of willfully going against an inner knowledge of what is right increases the idea of "I" and "mine."

When the soul chooses to go against that inner warning, a predictable set of consequences is set into motion. A series of inner states of mind emerge: shame, fear, jealousy, anger, and even murder. And, murder is not killing for food or self-protection, but due only to these new lower states of mind. The idea of a fall can only come from self-awareness that knows better. This means a self-awareness of good and bad and a freedom of will to go against what one knows to be right. This act of will completes the identification with "I" and "mine" and seals off the connection with the Creator. This is the fall of the human. Once some souls discover the apparent power of "I" and "mine," they go about indoctrinating newly emerging humans from the animal kingdom into this new ideal. Life after life reinforces the notion of separation from the Creator and the predominance of might makes "right" until it is an unquestioned belief. Life loses real Love and Joy.

Development of language, the study of mathematics, observation of the stars, systems of laws and other signals of higher intelligence gradually become more pronounced as the information produces more successful and stable societies. Philosophers question the human's place in creation; the whys and wherefores of existence challenge some of the great minds. Superstitions are debunked and reason gains more of a foothold. The development of ethics from the higher reasoning brain (Buddhi) works in competition with the wants and desires of Manas, making for many ethical challenges. The increasing body of human knowledge increases their dominance in the world and heightens the sense of safety and control. However, the development of reason without the guidance and the directional rudder of the pure vibration of the Holy Spirit (Chit) ultimately results in both an unstable human personality and society.

Gaining outward dominance does not produce the hoped-for bliss the earlier human had once thought it would. The development of higher reason is but a stepping-stone to something higher still. The reasoning mind, disappointed by the results of its worldly gains, is then turned inward to discover more fundamental truths of existence and the meaning of life (an important direction in the maze has been turned). An inner attraction draws the consciousness to realms beyond the Material World. This results in an inner illumination that transcends the reasoning mind. It taps directly into the intuitive apprehension of Truth (the Buddhi Mind illumined by the Holy Ghost). With this transcendent perception fresh in the mind, the soul begins its upward ascent in earnest in order to become established in higher Spiritual Consciousness.

In this ascension, the soul's upward pull from the Holy Ghost is intersected by the repulsion (Ahamkar) exerted by attachment to the body (Manas). This polarity represents the greatest potential for the fall of the human, for it is here that the soul can most profoundly turn away from its inner calling. When the desire for inner illumination draws the devotee to God, simultaneously, the temptation for earthly existence is very strongly felt. By turning away from the higher calling to God, humans push away the inner prompting for their own Awakening. This leads individuals further away from the light of their redemption—rather, into the maze and away from freedom.

As humans ascend this spinal stairway of consciousness, at each successive level the horizontal opposition of the worldly attraction seeks to deflect or turn downwards the upward Spiritual drive. The meeting of this oppositional energy and the overcoming of it is the Mystical Crucifixion. The horizontal worldly desires cross the vertical Spiritual energy coming up the spine and forms the cross at each one of these junctures: the heart, the throat, and the medulla.

Through overcoming each of these obstacles and drawing all energies up to the third eye point (the ajna or Kutastha Chaitanya), the world is seen as a dream and the inner Light is seen as the preeminent Reality (exit stage right). Through the overcoming of the lower mind (Manas) and the purification of the higher mind (Buddhi), the power of the Holy Spirit (Chit) magnetically draws the consciousness, and thereby the soul, back to its origins of pure God (Sat). The inner and outer Realities are now seen as one complete whole, as the Creator and creation are known to be one, without separation. This illumination leads humans out of the maze (Maya) and back to their origins of universal Love and Bliss. They are once again established in the Truth of their origin as Self—in absolute freedom as Sat Chid Ananda.

OM TAT SAT

References

Guillaumont, A; Puech, Henri; Quispel, W.; and Masih, Yassah; Translators. (1959). *The Gospel According to Thomas.*

Hickenbottom, David. (2019). *My Spiritual India.* Camano Island, Washington: The Cross and The Lotus Publishing.

Hickenbottom, David. (2021). *Climbing the Sacred Mountain: Poems and Prayers of a Western Yogi.* Camano Island, Washington: The Cross and The Lotus Publishing.

Hickenbottom, David. *Householder Yogi: Journal of a Western Yogi 2001–2002.* In development.

Kemp, Harry. (1925). *The Home Book of Modern Verse.* London: Henry Holt & Co.

Paramhansa Yogananda. (1946). *Autobiography of a Yogi.* New York: The Philosophical Library.

Paramhansa Yogananda. (1994). *Sayings of Paramhansa Yogananda.* Los Angeles, California: Self-Realization Fellowship.

Paramhansa Yogananda. (1995). *God Talks with Arjuna: Bhagavad Gita.* Los Angeles, California: Self-Realization Fellowship.

Sri Ramakrishna. Translator. Swami Nikhilananada. (1964). *The Gospel of Sri Ramakrishna.* Madras, India: Sri Ramakrishna Math.

Swami Sri Yukteswar Giri. (1949). *The Holy Science.* India: Yogoda Sat-Sang Society of India. 3rd Edition.

Bible References

King James Bible Online: https://www.kingjamesbibleonline.org

The Cross and The Lotus: www.crossandlotus.com

Editor's Acknowledgments

A beautiful thank you to Yogacharya David who asked me to assist him with publishing his teachings. Sadly, he left his body far too soon, before we could begin that endeavor. After David's passing, Carla, his devoted wife and disciple, invited me to organize and present David's brilliant writings, his modern-day views of a Western Yogi, in text form, for all to benefit. It is a privilege to work with David's legacy—teachings designed to support wise stewardship in today's world.

My thanks to Rebecca Harvey; her keen eye ensured that we caught details. Much appreciated. Zia Cole, my editor, polished all our hard work, refining the manuscript.

Gratitude to Jan Westendorp of Kato Design who used her creative talents to bring us this beautiful book, featuring David's teachings in the best possible manner.

David's image portfolio provided us with all the images, and Mike Victory, with his highly professional photography skills, has ensured that each image looks its best—including the cover image of David at Cloud Mountain.

My appreciation to Reverend Larry Koler and his wife, Cate Koler, from The Cross and The Lotus Publishing. They answered my questions and shared their knowledge while ensuring that the book was published in a timely fashion.

www.ingramcontent.com/pod-product-compliance
Lightning Source LLC
Chambersburg PA
CBHW070918120626
46546CB00001B/307